CARRINGTON
A LIFE AND A POLICY

CARRINGTON
A LIFE AND A POLICY

Patrick Cosgrave

J. M. Dent & Sons Ltd
London Melbourne

First published 1985
© Patrick Cosgrave 1985

This book is set in 11/13½ VIP Sabon by
D. P. Media Limited, Hitchin, Hertfordshire

Printed in Great Britain by
Richard Clay (The Chaucer Press) Ltd,
Bungay, Suffolk, for
J. M. Dent & Sons Ltd
Aldine House, 33 Welbeck Street, London W1M 8LX

ISBN 0-460-04691-8

This one is for Michael Shaw
who kept the faith.

CONTENTS

1. The Beginning   1
2. The Fall   16
3. The Peer   42
4. The Difficulty   65
5. The Defence of the Realm   86
6. The Office   113
7. The Record   139
8. The Aftermath   162

Index   177

LIST OF ILLUSTRATIONS

1. The 37-year-old High Commissioner to Australia.
2. En route to the Radcliffe Commission in February 1963.
3. As Leader of the Opposition in the House of Lords, 1969.
4. The Shadow Cabinet on 20 May 1970.
5. With Dr Helmut Schmidt in Bonn, 15 June 1970.
6. Taking part in a NATO exercise, 24 July 1973.
7. With Dr Josef Luns and Mr Dom Mintoff, 1972.
8. Carrington speaks, Heath listens: Conservative Party Conference, Blackpool, October 1973.
9. Sponsoring Sir Alec Douglas-Home in the House of Lords.
10. Applauded for a speech on Rhodesia at the Conservative Party Conference in October 1979.
11. When Rhodesia became Zimbabwe.
12. Lord Carrington attentive, Mrs Indira Ghandi pensive: January 1980 in New Delhi.
13. Leaving No 10, 2 June 1980, after a Cabinet debate on the contribution of the United Kingdom to the budget of the EEC.
14. A celebration to mark the creation of Zimbabwe, 19 April 1980.
15. The Secretary-General of NATO holds forth on his appointment.

NOTE

The Department of State of which Lord Carrington became chief after the general election of 1979 is, properly speaking, called the Foreign and Commonwealth Office. Its correct abbreviation is, therefore, FCO.

However, most of its members, supporters and critics, and most of those commenting on its activities continue to refer to it as the Foreign Office, the Office, or the FO. In the necessarily multitudinous references to it in the following pages I have followed their practice.

So far, however, on the hard evidence, the peace-maker may have to rethink his philosophy, for the two wars have shown that good is not automatically blessed, and that security is not guaranteed by good intentions. Quite the contrary, for conciliation, negotiation, compromise, tolerance – all the civilized words in the Christian and democratic vocabulary – have too often turned out to be a trap. It is doubtless to the credit of man that he has sought a better way to keep the peace than that of alliances, and the balance of power by promoting organizations dedicated to supplying security through an International Police Force; but trust in the League of Nations turned out to be misplaced, and the United Nations so far has no relevance in the setting of the rivalry of great powers. Neither Covenants nor Charters have been able to guarantee peace.

Lord Home of the Hirsel,
Letters to a Grandson (London 1983).

1. THE BEGINNING

So time that is o'er kind
　　To all that be,
Ordains us e'en as blind,
　　As bold as she:
That in our very death,
　　And burial sure,
Shadow to shadow, well-persuaded, saith,
　　'See how our works endure!'

Rudyard Kipling, a poem in preface to
'A Centurion of the Thirtieth',
from *Stalky and Co*

In the opening chapter of that splendid book *Curzon: the last phase*[1] Sir Harold Nicolson expresses, explicitly as well as by implication, the view of George Curzon, first Marquis Curzon of Kedleston, Viceroy of India and Secretary of State for Foreign Affairs, as a summation, an encapsulation, of a political culture – the imperial – which was entering its twilight. Nicolson's opening pages describe, in the limpid prose of which he was master, Curzon's address to the House of Lords on 18 November 1918, congratulating the Crown upon the surrender of the German, Austro-Hungarian and Ottoman Empires and their allies in the war just over.

Nicolson's view that a single individual, and particularly a politician, could state or summarise in himself the character of a policy, let alone a period of history, is far less certainly held nowadays than it was when he wrote, in 1934. To be sure, much history is still written in terms of personality, and there is a public still avid for the most recondite biographies of Hitler, and the most cavalier of Churchill. But it is the literary, rather than the political historians who most confidently state that their individual subjects – artists – can and do represent a period and reflect its character. 'He is one of those', read the Nobel Prize citation to Ernest Hemingway, 'who, honestly and

1. London, 1934, p. 1f.

— 1 —

undauntedly, reproduces the genuine features of the hard countenance of the age.' Historians of politics are, nowadays, a great deal more cautious.

Certainly, political biography still enjoys popular esteem. But the broad thrust of historical research is towards the searching out of anonymous, or pseudonymous trends, alongside the unravelling thread of which a personality or personalities fitfully march.

I do not say that this preference in the study and analysis of past events for the trend rather than for the individual is universal. Martin Gilbert's magisterial volumes – amounting to many thousands of pages – on Churchill are now nearing a triumphal conclusion, and it is barely possible, on any one of those pages, to escape the impress of the subject's personality. Dr John Barnes and Professor Keith Middlemas justified devoting comfortably more than one thousand pages to the life of Stanley Baldwin by saying[2]

> In many cases it is undesirable for political biography also to be the history of the subject's time – indeed it is the besetting sin. But in Baldwin's case it is almost inevitable and the authors can only apologise to readers familiar with the detailed story of the period.

In other words, say Barnes and Middlemas, the story of the man's life is intrinsically interesting, but to understand it you have to be told the story of the times as well: there is an implicit fissure here, a hint that there are two honourable subjects, biographies of men and histories of subjects, and that they should not, always, or even often, be told together. We have come a long way indeed from the Victorian – and pre-Victorian – idea of a book about somebody or other's 'Life and Times'. And even Martin Gilbert, for whose lavish provision of documentation in the companion volumes to his substantive account of Churchill's life[3] students will for generations be grateful, emphasises the man in his main text, and the times in the selected documents.

Yet even the most determinist of historians will admit that the

2. Keith Middlemas and John Barnes, *Baldwin: a biography* (London, 1969) p. xiv.
3. Dr Gilbert, in continuation of a work begun by Randolph Churchill, who wrote two volumes, has now reached volume six of his *magnum opus*. Each volume of text is accompanied by further substantial volumes of archival material.

presence of an individual, and his or her decision, may determine the outcome of an issue at a given moment. It is widely agreed, for example, à propos of an event crucial in the following pages, that the United Kingdom would not, in 1982, have fought for the Falkland Islands – the Task Force would not have sailed – had any other *conceivable* Prime Minister been at the governmental helm. Again, in 1940, had any other Conservative minister than Churchill held the supreme office of government, it is possible, if not probable, that this country would have made peace with Germany.[4] The determinist historian, however, considers such moments to be exceptions rather than rules in the great unfolding of the historical process; and he is convinced that the greatest concession that the search for truth can make to the study of personality is to admit the moderate significance of a personal intervention in a chain of events. Thus, it is unlikely that Lord Carrington would have become Foreign Secretary or even, perhaps, Leader of the House of Lords, had a particular chain of events not occurred in 1963. The links in that chain were, first, the coming into force of legislation introduced by Harold Macmillan under the provisions of which a peer could resign his title and become available to stand for election to the House of Commons; then the illness of Harold Macmillan, which forced his resignation as Prime Minister; the (successful) intrigue mounted by Macmillan from his hospital bed to secure the succession to himself of Lord Home;[5] and the decision of Lord Hailsham to renounce his peerage in order to contest that succession.

Success in any political career depends on a large admixture of good fortune in any combination of talent and ambition. But Carrington was fortunate beyond the normal measure, surely, by being in the right place at the time of the extraordinary, and even bizarre events that characterised the Conservative leadership crisis of October 1963.

Consider. Lord Home's active political career did not end until the defeat of the Conservative government in the general election of February 1974, and Lord Hailsham's continues as I write. But the

4. See Patrick Cosgrave, *Churchill at war: alone* (London, 1974) pp. 211f.
5. There is a substantial literature on the subject of the succession to the Conservative leadership in 1963. The most recent summaries are to be found in Patrick Cosgrave, *R. A. Butler: an English life* (London, 1981) pp. 131f and Nigel Fisher, *Harold Macmillan* (London, 1982) pp. 334f.

service of both men in the Upper House was interrupted by their decisions in October 1963, and into the breach that their departure for the other place left in Conservative ranks in 1963 Peter Carrington stepped. His new position made the prospect of senior Cabinet office far more than a dream. Had both men stayed where they were he would, no doubt, given his ability and charm, have held office in future Conservative governments, but it would have been unlikely to have been office of the first rank. For, though Tory are more likely than Labour Prime Ministers to appoint peers to major government posts, even they, particularly as the century marches steadily on, feel, insensibly, that the numbers of such appointments should be kept severely down (though there is no constitutional prohibition on the holding of any government office, including that of Prime Minister, save that of Chancellor of the Exchequer, by a member of the House of Lords).

Home and Hailsham having departed, however, Carrington was the natural, perhaps the only candidate for the leadership of his party in the Lords. And, though his stewardship in that position gives rise to serious questioning of his political judgement[6] he was, when Edward Heath won the 1970 general election, an obvious candidate for high office: he became Secretary of State for Defence. He was to suffer disappointment later. Not least because of his own poor advice Heath appealed to the country in February 1974, and lost the ensuing two electoral battles, falling victim himself to the ambitions of Margaret Thatcher in 1975. Carrington feared — and his friends feared even more strongly for him — that his closeness to Heath would ensure his exclusion from a Cabinet post of real importance in the event of Mrs Thatcher ever forming a government. 'The sad thing about it all', said a friend and acolyte of his to me in the middle of 1975, when we were discussing the Thatcher victory in the leadership battle of that year, 'is that we've lost for ever the possibility of having a really first-class, a great, Foreign Secretary.' However, on her own general election victory in 1979, and in part at least in recognition of his loyal and resumed service as Leader in the Lords between 1975 and 1979, Margaret Thatcher gave Carrington his heart's desire, the position of

6. See David Butler and Denis Kavanagh, *The British General Election of February 1974* (London, 1974) pp. 27f.

Her Majesty's Principal Secretary of State for Foreign Affairs. None of this would have occurred had it not been for the precipitate breaking of a noble log-jam in October 1963. At best, had Macmillan's resignation, with all that flowed from it, not happened then Carrington could have looked forward to dignified, but hardly significant political employment, part of the necessary, but hardly crucial balance in the structure of government. Instead he went on to climb heights relatively dizzy for a peer and, in 1982, to suffer a commensurate fall.

I invoked, earlier, the name and history of Curzon, as Harold Nicolson saw his story, and I propose to argue that they represented something – a tradition – in an unusual, even an exceptional way, and in a way not dissimilar to that of Carrington. Curzon, Nicolson tells us,[7] when still a boy, wrote his own epitaph in which his achievements of the offices of Viceroy of India, Secretary of State for Foreign Affairs and Prime Minister were all recorded, and that aggressive combination of flamboyance and certainty – which often sat ill with the uncertainty and diffidence which were likewise parts of his character – is central to our understanding of Curzon. Peter Carrington may shudder at the vulgarity, not so much of the triple ambition itself as of its expression, but there is something alike about the two men, none the less.

Curzon was conscious – perhaps over-conscious – of his abilities; and, for all that his career ended in final failure, he did achieve the first two of the goals he had set himself. Those abilities, as he thought, entitled him to entertain the very highest of ambitions, the reward of which would not be glory merely, but the opportunity to render service. Carrington, however, is made on an altogether more modest scale. In his time it was, in practical terms, impossible for a man to be Prime Minister and remain in the House of Lords, and he always preferred the certainty of his peerage to the chances of electoral politics. Thus, he was amazed at the decisions of Home and Hailsham in 1963. 'I just couldn't understand,' he observed not long after the event, 'what Alec and Quintin thought they were up to. Imagine *wanting* to be a member of the House of Commons.' There was a twinkle in the eye when he said it, and that twinkle, which accompanies most of his pronouncements, and which serves both as a genuine

7. Nicolson, *op. cit.*, p. 353.

expression of humour and as a matter of concealment, was there *de haut en bas*.

Be all that as it may, however, Carrington was clear from the very early age at which he succeeded to his father's title both that he wanted to be a politician and that he did not want to seek a seat in the House of Commons. The ability of peers to disclaim their titles was secured through the doughty campaign of Lord Stansgate (later Anthony Wedgwood Benn and, subsequently, Tony Benn) who was determined to build his career in the Lower House. But once the necessary legislation had been passed, disclamation, without becoming the order of the day, enjoyed, for a time, a certain fashion. There were those, like Lord Beaverbrook (Sir Maxwell Aitken) and Lord Fraser of Allander (Sir Hugh Fraser) who disclaimed out of an interesting and touching respect for their fathers, expressed in Aitken's remark, 'There can never be more than one Lord Beaverbrook so far as I'm concerned.' There were men of parts (aside from Benn) who disclaimed in the interests of a Commons career, like Lord Altrincham (John Grigg), the Earl of Sandwich (Victor Montagu) and the Earl of Durham (Lord Lambton): the first two failed in their endeavour because they could not acquire parliamentary nominations, and the third saw his ministerial career destroyed by scandal. A handful of peers, further, disclaimed because of their disapproval of the House of Lords as an institution, or for other personal reasons. While it was feared by some constitutionalists in 1963, however, that the relevant act would lead to a destructive exodus of political talent from the Lords, the vast majority stayed where they were, among them, of course, Carrington.

The difference between Carrington and most of those who took the same position as he did was his desire – his ambition – not just to hold office, but to hold high office. Every government, of whatever colour, requires a leavening of peers and, as I have already observed, a Conservative government offers greater opportunities for advancement than does a Labour administration. But the developing fashion of the period since 1955 (Churchill's last government having had an almost top-heavy look about it, deriving from the number of members of the House of Lords holding important offices and heading great departments of state) has dictated that peers should, in the main, be confined to the lower reaches of the governmental slope. Even in 1985, with a Prime Minister less inclined to follow fashion in these matters than her recent predecessors or likely successors, peers like Lord Gowrie (in charge of the arts) or Lord Young (entrusted with a roving commission of unemployment and trade) do not head major departments. Fashion, in these matters, follows practicality: the House of Commons is the legislative body which commands the purse, and it has the last word in the survival or otherwise of a government. Its members do not take kindly to the presence in council of powerful ministers whom it cannot question. When Harold Macmillan appointed the Earl of Home as Foreign Secretary the murmur of criticism approached a shout. When, in April 1982, Argentina having invaded the Falkland Islands, the Commons savaged the record of his department on this issue, Carrington, unable to reply to criticism he felt to be unjustified in the chamber in which it was made, felt obliged to resign. The constitutional position in which he found himself was not his only reason for resignation – when he said 'I felt it would lance the boil' he was probably giving the most important reason – but it was one that had considerable personal weight.

Carrington's ambitions were always understated, and the modesty which was their cloak became even more marked after the events of 1963 thrust him into much greater prominence than he might, in other circumstances, have enjoyed. Richard Crossman, for example, found him both pliant and unassertive in matters concerning the reform of the House of Lords.[8] He records one occasion on which he was amazed by Carrington's ready concession to the Labour government on the matter of the delaying powers that the Upper House was to have after legislation,[9] and another occasion on which Carrington expressed pessimism at the prospect of his being able to convince Edward Heath and the Conservative Shadow Cabinet of the desirability of acceeding to Crossman's proposals.[10] 'He said,' reports Crossman, ' "It's no good talking to me, you should go personally to Heath and explain it all to him." '

What was always clear to those who observed Carrington in action, after he had reached the forefront of high politics, was that, along with

8. Richard Crossman, *The Diaries of a Cabinet Minister*, Volume iii (ed. Janet Morgan, London, 1977) p. 233.
9. Richard Crossman, *The Diaries of a Cabinet Minister*, Volume ii (ed. Janet Morgan, London, 1976) p. 523.
10. *Ibid.* p. 526.

his wry, humorous modesty – the aristocratic nonchalance which was so much a part of his public demeanour – and the hard ambition which lay beneath it, went a stubborn certitude about many matters of public concern and an unforced willingness to fight his corner. What Crossman saw as a surprising pliancy covered a settled conviction that, considered as a political institute, the House of Lords was hopelessly out of date, and that a failure to institute substantial reforms would speed the march towards its abolition. It is not necessary to agree with this proposition – and, twenty years on, the House of Lords looks a great deal more secure both in its remaining powers and in public esteem than would have seemed imaginable in the 1960s – to appreciate the strength with which he held to it. Again, in relation to a subject – the repeated necessity of re-imposing sanctions on the rebel Smith government in Rhodesia[11] – which plagued him continuously in and out of office, he showed a repeated willingness – indeed determination – to go against the grain of party sentiment. In no sense, therefore, at any time in his career has Peter Carrington sought to compensate for his lack of a popular base by currying favour with members of the Conservative Party through the adoption of populist positions on matters of policy.

The iron in the man was all the less noticed because of his manner. A civil servant who had worked in both of their private offices made an instructive contrast between Carrington and his Labour predecessor, Dr David Owen. 'With David', he said, 'it was go, go, go all the time. That's the sense in which he is so like Margaret Thatcher. Everything was done in a rush, and he took the view that it should, anyway, have been done yesterday. With Peter we found that we could *stroll* again. This didn't mean that work was neglected. I've never had a minister who worked harder. But there was no atmosphere of frenzy about the office. This led some people to think that he was languid, but he wasn't: he just enjoyed appearing to be.'

Indeed, there is a great deal of evidence to show the tougher sides of Carrington's character, which I will discuss later. For the moment, however, it is sufficient – as it is necessary – to stress the importance to

11. Mr Ian Smith's Rhodesian government declared unilateral independence from Britain in 1965. This action was followed by the imposition of economic sanctions by every member country of the United Nations except South Africa. The sanctions were, however, only fitfully implemented.

him of the controlled image with which he faced the world. With the –
in style, at least – not dissimilar Alec Douglas-Home the observer felt
that the relaxed, almost detached approach to public affairs, and
particularly to political crisis, was, so to speak, almost bred in the
bone: it came from being a fourteenth earl rather than a sixth baron.
With Carrington, especially in moments of stress, the style seemed
contrived, and perhaps even sustained by an exceptional act of will. If
this is so, however, the cloak was donned early, for those who served
with him in the Army sketch the same lineaments of personality as do
those who were later to observe him as a politician.

For instance, he is often amusingly deprecating about the origins of
his title, his banker ancestors having been first raised to the peerage in
1796 by way of an Irish title which did not carry with it the right to a
seat in the House of Lords, an omission which was repaired in the
following year. Partly, no doubt from a sound sense of wise personal
tactics in his relations with Margaret Thatcher, but partly also because
of a genuine sense of something missing in his equipment for government, he steadily refused to be drawn into discussion on economic
policy either in the Shadow Cabinet from 1975 to 1979 or in the
Cabinet between 1979 and 1982. It was known, of course, that he had
instinctive doubts about the rightness of the policies adopted after the
1979 victory. Indeed, his number two at the Foreign Office, Sir Ian
Gilmour (who had been his strongly urged personal preference for that
position, having also a seat in the Cabinet as Lord Privy Seal), became
perhaps the leading critic of the Prime Minister within Conservative
ranks and the two men were more than normally close. When
Gilmour's increasingly open attacks led to his dismissal from the
government Carrington was saddened; but nothing would make him
break ranks with the Prime Minister.

The closeness of Carrington to Mrs Thatcher has been exaggerated
– there was, for instance a marked contrast between the coldness of
her letter to him accepting his resignation in 1982 and the warmth of
her missive to John Nott, the Secretary of State for Defence, refusing
his – but it was obvious enough to be one of the chief features of the
1979 government. It was enough, further, to make her assiduous in
her search for alternative employment of sufficient status for him after
the war for the Falklands was over, a search which ended when he
became Secretary-General of NATO. The closeness, moreover,

survived what might have been an intolerable strain, the Prime Minister's deep-rooted and ineradicable suspicion of the Foreign Office itself.

The very special nature of the position that the Foreign Office occupies in the structure of British political society is discussed below, in Chapter 6. An understanding of that position, and an understanding of the particular felicity of the relations between department and chief from 1979 onwards, is vital to any examination of Peter Carrington's rôle in British political history. The possession, however, by the Office of a special place in the machinery of government, and the existence of that felicity, make it all the more remarkable that personal relations between Foreign Secretary and Prime Minister remained so good for so long. There were, to be sure, differences. Incorrigibly suspicious of all institutions, and particularly of the Civil Service, the Prime Minister delights in the most painstaking and vigilant criticism of departmental actions, from the trivial to the most significant. Her attitude to the Foreign Office is particularly unsparing and even Carrington did not always himself escape the lash of her tongue. On one occasion, for example, when she detected an error in a lengthy Office briefing and pounced on it with glee, Carrington, not unreasonably, made a remark to the effect that an error in a long paper was hardly of major importance. 'It wasn't', she said in full Cabinet, 'just an error. It was incompetence, and it came from the very top.'

Now, Margaret Thatcher's whole style of conversation, her whole method of conducting business, is an essentially combative one. Attack is in the very air she breathes, and six years in office – following more than four as Leader of the Opposition – have in no way dulled her capacity for amazement when it subsequently appears that rhetorical lashing out on her part has given offence, needlessly or unfairly. The most urbane – and loyal – of colleagues have found this a trying aspect of her personality, and matters were often especially hard for Carrington because so much of her dislike and disapprobation was focused so tightly on his department. Yet it was rare in the extreme for him to show resentment.

An unshakeable, if unstated, self-esteem is one of the vital parts of Carrington's armour, and, for all that it lives with some inner uncertainties and resentments, it undoubtedly provided him with some protection from the various sallies of the Prime Minister. He has allowed himself, even, to reply with remarks that if not exactly barbed, were at least edged. Thus, when asked on television that old chestnut of a question that all political journalists trot out at some point in conversation with any senior politician, the question that runs, 'If the Prime Minister were run over by a bus, then who . . . ?,' his reply was instant: 'The bus wouldn't dare.' It was said lightly, even affectionately, but there was a sharpness to it, and it very accurately conveyed the not always admiring appreciation by Mrs Thatcher's colleagues of the whirlwind side of her personality.

There was, however, something else lying behind both his success in cultivating an amicable relationship with her and his resolute eschewing of any intervention in matters of government outside his strict departmental brief. And that something else, I believe, goes far to justify my earlier description of him as an individual summarising and expressing in a profound, if not always conscious way a whole mode and tradition of politics. It can best be described as a sort of armoured reserve about his judgement and influence.

It was not just because he feels the lack of a univeristy degree, not just because he is unfeignedly honest about his ignorance on matters of economic policy, not just because he thought it tactically unwise in 1979 to express the reservations he had about the direction taken by an unusually forceful Prime Minister, that Carrington, from 1979 to 1982, so carefully restricted the range of his interventions in government business. There were at least two other reasons.

The first was his consciousness of his misjudgement of the national electoral situation in the closing weeks of 1973 and the opening weeks of 1974. At the time, as Douglas Hurd recalls,[12] the Prime Minister, Edward Heath, seemed stricken in gloom and lethargy: it was not known until much later that he was suffering from a thyroid deficiency which deprived him of energy. The battle between those who doubted the wisdom of an early appeal to the country and those who were eager for one ranged around his intellectually supine figure. William Whitelaw was prominent in the first camp, and Peter Carrington led the second. Carrington's advice was heeded; the government went down to defeat; and Heath was ultimately forced to vacate the leadership of the party. Carrington was acutely aware of the fact that he had

12. Douglas Hurd, *An end to promises: sketches of a government* (London, 1976).

misjudged a mood; although this consciousness did not affect his fundamental belief in himself.

The second reason for confining himself to his own diplomatic bailiwick during his time in office in the 1979 government was the fact that he had now reached the summit both of achievement and possibility. He had longed for – hungered after – the Foreign Office, and he was supremely content there. Any possible change of appointment would represent decline, not merely in the public estimation, but in his own. It was not simply that he would take no action outside his own area of responsibility that would put his position at risk, but that he felt uncommonly fulfilled where he was. An inner certainty that had always been an important part of his make-up became, in 1979, virtually the whole of it.

By 1979, again, Carrington had acquired for himself a substantial number of other distinctions, not necessarily of very great weight in themselves, but such as gave him considerable personal satisfaction. His Military Cross he had been awarded (for gallantry) in 1945. In 1958, after his stint as High Commissioner in Australia, he was dubbed KCMG. He became a Privy Councillor in 1959. He was an honorary member of the Royal Academy and its Secretary for foreign correspondence, as well as being Chairman of the Board of Trustees of the Victoria and Albert Museum. He was a Fellow of Eton and of St Antony's College, Oxford, while, finally, he had been awarded three honorary doctorates. His work at the Victoria and Albert and the Royal Academy was serious, and it was discharged conscientiously, but in the main his honours were those attaching to a man occupying a certain position in public life rather than distinctions given in reward for achievement or in the hope of return.

What Carrington felt he could, in 1979, do supremely well was to articulate and then implement – with grace and forensic skill – a foreign policy appropriate to a post-imperial country that had yet to decide precisely how she should adjust to an as-yet ill-fitting new partnership with the other medium-sized powers of continental Europe. Surprised, after her general election victory, to be given the real job by the new Prime Minister, he was, in addition, visited by a certain trepidation. She had, in opposition, shown herself to have exceptionally definite views in his own field, and particularly in the area of relations between the Western Alliance and the Soviet Union.

She was not, furthermore, an individual with any very noted taste for the niceties of diplomacy by which – as his post-Falklands denunciation of 'megaphone diplomacy' showed – he set considerable store.

Here again, however, circumstances and inclination alike gave him certain advantages. The attitude which, in opposition, Margaret Thatcher struck on the questions of what the USSR represented in international relations and what the Western response to it should be, influenced as it was by academic studies of Soviet policy and society,[13] rested in the first instance upon an exceptional impatience with what she and her supporters regarded as the excessively compliant tendency of traditional British diplomacy towards Soviet ambition, and a dangerous willingness to tread the (initially) primrose paths of appeasement in the form of détente. From his style Carrington might be thought to fall wholly into the traditional mould. But, again, it was not so. He had been, for most of the life of the Heath government of 1970–4, Secretary of State for Defence, and his experience in that job – where he was considered something of a hawk – had left him with few illusions on Soviet policy. He was to change somewhat during his period in office; but initially the prospects of instinctive agreement between himself and his Prime Minister were much greater than might have been supposed from a superficial glance in 1979.

Then it was an advantage to both of them that the first major foreign policy problem the new government had to deal with was that of the rebel colony of Rhodesia. Judgements now vary widely on the merits or otherwise of the settlement which turned that country into black-ruled Zimbabwe, and historically, as I argue below, the Prime Minister was far more responsible than has hitherto been allowed both for the initial switch of policy which opened the way to an agreement between all the participating powers and factions and for the shape of the settlement which was ultimately arrived at.[14] But the fact of the matter was that from the 1979 Commonwealth Prime Ministers' conference in Lusaka, through the constitutional conference at Lancaster House in London which followed it, to the triumph of Robert Mugabe in the Zimbabwean general election, Prime Minister and Foreign Secretary worked together not only closely but

13. See Patrick Cosgrave, *Thatcher: the first term* (London, 1985) pp. 50f.
14. Below, p. 144ff.

happily. The international amazement which greeted the emergence of a settlement to so protracted a conflict, and the accompanying waves of congratulation, bound them together in the public mind and in the estimation of each for the other. The serious differences which were implicit in their very different approaches to other problems did not, in the wake of the independence of Zimbabwe, become explicit enough to threaten that alliance, until Argentinians landed on the Falkland Islands.

The very special position that Carrington occupied in the first Thatcher administration therefore made him particularly a free agent as to attitude in policy and method in diplomacy.

He is not a man given either to abstract thought or to philosophising about political activity. As Foreign Secretary, however, he expressed a policy which had philosophical, or at least historical roots, roots which had been tenderly nursed in the Foreign Office since at least the Suez débâcle of 1956. These dictated, fundamentally, the concentration of British interest and effort within the Atlantic Alliance, on the European rather than the American side of the balance. Unlike any previous British Foreign Secretary (but like Edward Heath) he took this emphasis immensely seriously. As a consequence, although American interest in, and, in general, approval of Margaret Thatcher waxed with the years, Carrington was never popular on the other side of the Atlantic, and he has been compelled to work at the repair of damaged or broken bridges since becoming Secretary-General of NATO.

With the emerging Eurocentricity of policy went, of necessity, an impulsion to cut the remaining bonds of responsibility with the old Empire and the new Commonwealth. In debates in the House of Lords, and in other public utterances during the unravelling of the Rhodesian imbroglio, Carrington frequently displayed an impatient and abrasive side to his tongue. This aroused not only suspicion in Africa but also criticism at home among those who feared that the Thatcher government would not see its responsibilities through to the end in Rhodesia or who thought that a gentle and sympathetic approach was a *sine qua non* for handling black politicians. Even before the Lancaster House conference opened, and more dramatically on several occasions during its course, Carrington told those with whom he was negotiating that they could either take or leave a given

British offer. He wanted Britain to be as fair to all concerned as she could; but he was impatient to be gone. Likewise, and in the end for him tragically, he may have unwittingly encouraged Argentina to believe that the British interest in the Falklands was a very minor one indeed.

I have, in the following pages, concentrated far more on Peter Carrington as an executant of foreign policy than would be desirable in a full biography. That is not only because his tenure of the Foreign Office, and his stewardship of British diplomacy, constitute by far the most important part of his public life, but because he himself saw that tenure as infinitely the most significant and rewarding part of his life in politics. On the other hand, all that went before — his family background, his time in the Army, his emergence as a front-ranking politician in the House of Lords, his two spells in defence ministries, and his rise to a significant, if short-lived position of great influence in the Conservative Party — were parts of what made him the man he was in 1979. Conversely, his conduct in earlier jobs gives important clues to an understanding of how he set about official life in the most self-consciously radical Conservative government of the century.

2. THE FALL

They went to sea in a Sieve, they did
   In a Sieve they went to sea:
In spite of all their friends could say,
On a winter's morn, on a stormy day,
   In a Sieve they went to sea!
And when the Sieve turned round and round,
And every one cried, 'You'll all be drowned!'
They called aloud, 'Our Sieve ain't big,
'But we don't care a button! we don't care a fig!
   In a Sieve we'll go to sea!'

Edward Lear, 'The Jumblies', in *Nonsense Songs*

Between his appointment as Foreign Secretary in May 1979 and his resignation in April 1982 Carrington enjoyed an assured, if often hectic progress. His critics were few, and if they were bitter, their bile could count for little against the acclaim that assailed him from all sides. As we shall see, the smooth surface of his diplomacy, and his unruffled presentation of himself and his policy, concealed a number of points of danger and difficulty. From the election of President Ronald Reagan in 1980, for example, distrust of Carrington – though not of his Prime Minister – grew in Washington. In the foreign ministries and cabinets of the EEC countries there was confusion and suspicion about and of the policy of the British government: the Foreign Office appeared (in the continental eye) constructive and friendly, No 10 Downing Street obstructive and sometimes hostile. In the parliamentary Conservative Party there were, particularly among the most loyal supporters of Margaret Thatcher, those who viewed Lord Carrington with a doubtfulness verging on, and sometimes spilling over into, blatant hostility. The hard core of her supporters in the battle for the Conservative leadership in 1975 included all those who feared that the Foreign Office was all too ready to yield to the demands of the European Economic Community, and most of those who supported Israel in her confrontation with the Arab powers in the

Middle East. This latter group viewed with particular disfavour the fact that Carrington had chosen as his deputy in the House of Commons Sir Ian Gilmour, a founder member of the Council for the Advancement of Arab-British Understanding. It was later to appear to them an enjoyable irony that it was while on a visit to Israel that Carrington learned of the Falklands invasion that brought about his downfall.

Carrington's fall – his subsequent appointment as Secretary-General of NATO, though a compensation, could hardly be described as a new rise – was an intensely dramatic one. It is not mere hindsight to view his whole career in its light, for it is in his treatment of the events leading up to it, and of the event itself, that we can most clearly observe the essential characteristics of the man in his handling of public policy. His appointment in 1979 was the culmination of his career, but the fall in 1982, painful as it was, constituted as apt a summary of his characteristics and their consequences.

The date of the Argentinian invasion of the Falkland Islands was 2 April 1982, and thus the first major occasion in the history of what was to prove to be a remarkable campaign. But there were two earlier dates of intense significance, particularly so far as Carrington himself was concerned. The first was 11 December 1981, when General Leopoldo Fortunato Galtieri entered the Casa Rosada in Buenos Aires to be sworn in as President of his country and leader of Argentina's three-man military *junta*. The second was 30 March 1982. A few days previously Carrington had finished a trying session of EEC foreign ministers in Brussels, and Israel was next on his agenda. His visit there was not expected to be – from the point of view of European policy – a particularly constructive one. For some time the EEC governments had been trying to hammer out a policy of their own on the Middle East. They required that such a policy should have two interlocking features: it should be independent of the policy of the United States, and it should be even-handed as between Israel and the Arab powers. There was plenty of pro-Arab (or, perhaps, more correctly, pro-Palestinian Arab) sentiment in Western Europe, but the real reason behind the hope for a distinct and united policy was that it should demonstrate European (that is, EEC) separateness from the Americans. All this is important as part of the background to the situation Carrington found himself in at the end of March that year.

It may be questioned whether the whole attitude of which Carrington's trip to Israel was representative was a wise one. All but one member – the Republic of Ireland – of the European Economic Community were members of the North Atlantic Treaty Organisation. The life of that organisation depends on the sustenance provided by the United States. That fact was – and is – both accepted and resented by the European powers. Their resentment has more than once issued in attempts through the EEC (which has no collective military element in its make-up) to state a collective identity independent of the Atlantic Alliance. Carrington was himself enthusiastic about such attempts for, like his fellow foreign ministers, he saw such a coming-together of Western Europe as a vital part of the creation of a Western European identity in all fields of policy, economic, political and social, as well as diplomatic. The Middle East, that fraught segment of the world which attracts the attention and interference of virtually every member of the United Nations, for good reasons and bad alike, had for some years seemed to the Europeans an admirable area for the fulfilment of their ideological ambitions. Now, having a policy for the sake of having a policy, without any particular consideration for a nation's real interests, is a very dangerous way of proceeding.[1] The Israelis, moreover, secure in their own relationship with the United States – particularly with the Reagan government – were irritated rather than impressed or worried by this European intervention in their region, and they had no particular desire to entertain Lord Carrington. They also, because of their generation-long pursuit of Nazi war criminals in Latin America, possessed formidable sources of intelligence in that sub-continent.

It would be wrong to suggest that Carrington hoped for very much of a specific nature from his visit to Israel. To him it was in part the continuation of a process whereby Israel might be brought to the negotiating table and in part an exercise in public relations, by which he set great store. None the less, there seemed to some of his advisers cogent reasons for postponing the trip. British intelligence in Argentina was uncertain and inchoate, and subsequent investigation was to show that the raw material transmitted to London was inefficiently processed. But there were distinct signs – faithfully recorded

1. See Irving Kristol, 'Transatlantic Misunderstanding' in *Encounter*, March, 1985.

by journalists in Buenos Aires serving British newspapers, as well as by some British diplomats and serving officers in South America – that the Galtieri government was planning a *coup de main* against the Falkland Islands. When the suggestion was made to Carrington, however, that he should remain at his post in London he declined to accept it, and gave three reasons.

First, he thought that Argentinian posturing was no more than that: so many threats had been issued from the mainland against the integrity of the islands that one more hardly made a crisis. Second, he considered that his visit to Israel was itself an event of some importance, as a step in the evolution of a common European policy on the Middle East. Third, he was convinced that any postponement of his trip would itself exacerbate the situation in the South Atlantic: it was important, he felt, to continue with business as usual. Psychologically, in the view of one of his predecessors as Foreign Secretary, this last was most important to him. He found it hard – and the next few days were to show how hard he found it – to imagine that a civilised and pro-Western country such as Argentina would take up arms against another Western country with which she had long-established ties over a trifling argument about who owned some islands in the South Atlantic. Like all his recent predecessors, he had had frequent and fruitless exchanges with Argentinian ministers on the future of the islands. Again, like his predecessors, he had been baulked more than once by opinion in the House of Commons which resisted the (to him) good sense of being accommodating to Argentinian ambitions. But he could not see a *casus belli* in the whole business. So he flew to Tel Aviv.

The Israeli reaction, not simply to Lord Carrington's visit, but to his arrival, was a mixed one.[2] Knowing its purpose they were, from their point of view, irritated by the visit. But they were also surprised that it was undertaken at all. At the beginning of the week, indeed, when I lunched with a senior Israeli diplomat, he told me with confidence that the Middle Eastern visit would be put off. I quoted back at him an assurance I had already received to the contrary. He was baffled. 'Don't your people appreciate,' he said with a certain amount of wonder, 'that you've got a major crisis building up in the South Atlantic? Or don't you care any more?' We both had already heard

2. Private information.

that the Prime Minister and the Foreign Secretary had, that Monday morning, en route to Brussels, decided to despatch three nuclear-powered submarines to take station off the Falklands: we did not know that none of the designated craft could sail immediately – HMS *Spartan* sailed within two days, *Splendid* followed her on 1 April, and *Conqueror* three days later, but, even so, *Spartan* was not on station until 12 April – nor did we know that the First Sea Lord, Sir Henry Leach, had called a staff operations meeting for that afternoon at the Ministry of Defence. Leach has since disclaimed the plaudits subsequently heaped on his shoulders for his prevision. 'Put it this way,' said one of those present on Monday, 'Henry wanted to be ready if an attack happened and the politicians decided to fight. He also decided, in about half an hour, that the full, or practically the full, resources of the Royal Navy would be needed to *guarantee* victory. And he reckoned that if he could practically guarantee victory to the Prime Minister, given her temperament, the chances of our doing something about an invasion would be that much greater.' It was also, and preponderantly, true that Leach, like many other sailors, bitterly resented the drastic cuts in naval provision foreshadowed in John Nott's various pronouncements on defence policy, and particularly disliked the strategic proposal to reduce the Navy essentially to an anti-submarine rôle in the North Sea. If a clear political imperative for action in the South Atlantic was shown, if it was shown, further, that his ships could meet it – that, in a word, an ocean-going capacity was still a desirable part of British strategy – then further prospects were brighter than they had hitherto seemed.

For all that the interests of his own service may have been at the front of Leach's mind, he was at least readier than anybody else to consider the possibility – indeed, the near-certainty – of an Argentinian attack: 'He reads the *Daily Telegraph*', said one of his admiring subordinates, soon after the Task Force had sailed. That paper, in the person of its Buenos Aires correspondent, Tony Allen-Mills, had for some time been more positive about the aggressive character of Argentinian intentions. There was a murmur of threat throughout Fleet Street; but the *Daily Telegraph* was firmer about it than any other paper, having the good fortune to employ a correspondent at once distinguished, confident in his judgement, and well-informed. It was taken amiss at the Foreign Office that William Deedes, the editor of the paper, gave so much credence and prominence to Allen-Mills's views. Deedes was, after all, a former Cabinet minister (in the government of Harold Macmillan) and a Privy Councillor, and it was thought that he should be more discreet. 'Bill, of all people,' said a senior diplomat in disgust, 'to be going in for sensationalism! I'd have thought better of him.' This remark – typical of many made throughout March – summarises the closed and optimistic world of the policy-makers at the time: what proved to be true was dubbed sensationalism, because the alternative did not bear thinking about. Deedes, tending to disbelieve though he did, made an editorial judgement based on the record of his reporter. 'He's always been right before,' he was reported to have said, 'why not now?'

On the flight to Brussels, according to one of those accompanying the Prime Minister and Carrington, little time was devoted to the question of the Falklands. 'That's the trouble', said one of those on the journey, 'there's *never* enough time.' The decision was quickly taken to send the submarines. Some politicians and civil servants were aware, if only vaguely, of the fact that, when a similar threat had blown up in 1977, the Callaghan government had positioned a task force just below the horizon. When this was revealed in the House of Commons in April 1982 much scepticism was expressed. If the ships were below the horizon, it was said, how could the Argentinians have seen them as an expression of British willingness to fight for the islands, particularly as no ultimatum, or even warning, had been issued? It later emerged, however, that Sir Maurice Oldfield, the head of the Secret Intelligence Service ('C'), had taken the trouble quietly to pass the word in Buenos Aires that the United Kingdom was in a position effectively to deal immediately with aggression. British interests were thus served. Argentinian *amour propre* was not offended. Peace reigned again.[3] Alas, however, complacency was encouraged.

On the Monday flight Carrington had, in any event, other matters on his mind. The forthcoming visit to Israel, though it ranked higher than the developing situation in the South Atlantic, was not the most important of them. What deeply, and even desperately, concerned him was the deteriorating state of relations between Britain and the other

3. Max Hastings and Simon Jenkins, *The Battle for the Falklands* (London, 1983), p. 51.

members of the European Economic Community. Matters had not gone well since Margaret Thatcher's election.[4] Carrington, like all of his advisers, was convinced that the Prime Minister was over-inclined to excitability on the subject of budgetary relations with the EEC. By boldness and obstinacy – against Foreign Office advice – she had, in 1979 and 1980, secured certain financial undertakings from her partners. These had not been fulfilled and were, in any event, designed only to satisfy need and demand over a limited period. In Mrs Thatcher's judgement further hectoring would both produce the financial rebates promised and get the Community well on the road to a fundamental reform of the budgetary structure such as would eliminate the need for the debilitating annual quarrels about money which had become such a regular feature of her first term.

Carrington disagreed. Her domineering rhetorical style, he accepted, had considerable domestic political advantages. When she said, at Strasbourg in 1979, 'I cannot play Sister Bountiful to the Community while my own electorate are being asked to forego improvements in the fields of health, education, welfare and the rest,' he could, like her, appreciate the thrill of satisfaction at blunt defiance that ran through the Conservative Party and – less strongly, but still truly – through the country. He was even prepared to admit – as he told a member of his private office – that, against expectations, her hard line in 1979 and 1980 had, to some extent at least, worked. He now thought, however, that the time had come for conciliation and a softer voice.

There were two strands in his thinking. In the first place he saw the future of Britain linked irrevocably with the Community. National interest had to be stated, even asserted. But there was, however cloudy its lineaments, a common interest without which the national interest could not itself prosper and which, in time, might come to be seen as having a greater substance than the national interest itself. The Prime Minister, he knew, did not share that vision or concern. There was no emotional rope linking her to continental concerns of the kind that regularly impelled her to utter even fulsome praise of the United States. She would, when it was required of her, say – 'parrot', would, perhaps, be a better verb – the conventionally acceptable things about her

4. Below, p. 154ff.

country's commitment to the new Europe. But there were few who were prepared to believe that hers was a more than formal tribute. Certainly, as Carrington knew only too well, the continental heads of government were not prepared to believe it. And it was his judgement that a plea for sympathy and understanding on budgetary matters would meet with a readier response than would a continuation of what, in 1979, the then Irish Prime Minister, Jack Lynch, had described as 'bullying, no more and no less'. Carrington had thus set himself, generally, but especially in the last week of March, to achieving the overall and vital objective of restraining the Prime Minister.

In the second place there was something about her which, as he put it, 'gives me the collywobbles'. By means of a series of blatant hints, delivered both in the House of Commons and more publicly, and particularly by her constant reiteration of the proposition that the cash she wanted back from the EEC was 'our money', Mrs Thatcher conveyed the impression that, *in extremis*, she would simply refuse to authorise the signing of the cheques representing the United Kingdom's agreed – under treaty – contributions of the European budget. She had, indeed, teased Cabinet, parliament, public, and other EEC governments about her plans in the event of a failure to meet her wishes. She had even encouraged – though the suggestion was his – a member of her staff to draw up a bill, in amendment of the Act of Parliament which had brought Britain into the EEC in the first place, which would make legal any decision to renege on treaty-ordained payments to Brussels. In Carrington's view such conduct was reckless, and her delight in it offensive. The fact that she had been speaking admiringly of the occasion when President de Gaulle had brought the whole Community to a halt in the service of French interests gave no pleasure either in Paris or at the Foreign Office.

'I'm looking forward to Israel, after this,' Carrington said towards the end of the Brussels meeting. Nothing had gone disastrously wrong, and the storm clouds of the South Atlantic had, it seemed, receded. None the less, paper flowed, even as far as Brussels, to Prime Minister and Foreign Secretary alike. There was a distinct thrumming offstage. The Italian Foreign Minister – knowledgeable about Argentina because of the substantial number of citizens of that country who had Italian connections, and because of extensive trade links between the two countries – asked Carrington if he was worried, and if there was anything Italy could do. He was, in a polite and even friendly, but certainly breezy fashion brushed off. When the exchanges at Brussels had been concluded, therefore, Prime Minister and Foreign Secretary alike, while concerned about impending events over the Falkland Islands, had agreed that the precautions they had taken – in the sending of the submarines – were probably sufficient to meet the needs of the moment. Talk at Brussels, when it had not been about the EEC budget, had been about the possibility of a European initiative in the Middle East, Carrington's next port of call. None the less, disturbing signals from the Government Communications Headquarters at Cheltenham, charged with the monitoring of the overseas intelligence communications of foreign powers, had penetrated even to the Belgian capital. The political air, even if it was not crackling, was disturbed.

It is necessary to repeat, however, the very general conviction that nothing would happen. It was agreed that the Argentinian government had been rattling their sabres; but it was not thought that they would be withdrawn from their scabbards. Nevertheless, it is right and just to say that the Joint Intelligence Committee (chaired by the deputy head of the Foreign Office, and attended by all the relevant heads of security departments) which met on Wednesday, 31 March should have seen what was coming. And one can say that Carrington, having communicated with the American Secretary of State, Alexander Haig, on 28 March seeking American intervention to restrain General Galtieri, should not, then, have set off for Tel Aviv. Yet it is fair to add that both Carrington and Richard Luce, the junior Foreign Office Minister in the House of Commons, told Parliament that week that *Endurance* – the armed Antarctic survey ship – which had been due for recall, would stay off the Falklands. And the fact of the matter was that even the sharpest critics of the conduct of British diplomacy had not fully grasped that the Galtieri government was really going to strike.

On the Monday afternoon, for example, my Israeli friend and I strolled, after our lunch, into High Street, Kensington. We shook hands, he about to turn right for his Embassy, I left for the tube train that would take me home. I thanked him for lunch. He held onto my hand for a moment longer than was necessary, and spoke intently. 'You do realise,' he said, 'that the Argies will be in the Falklands by the end of the week? That's not a guess. It's a fact.' When I reached home I made some telephone calls and found that the general opinion of my contacts was that, while the situation was far more serious than it had seemed earlier in the month, it was not yet critical: time was still available in which Argentina could be persuaded, or compelled, to back down. To this day, indeed, the American Central Intelligence Agency believes that a final decision to go ahead was not made by the Galtieri *junta* until the Wednesday of that week.

The response of the British government, and particularly of the Foreign Office, over the few days that separated the Brussels summit from the actual Argentinian landings, is full of interest, and it is as revealing of long-nurtured diplomatic method as it is of psychological expectations.

Max Hastings and Simon Jenkins have described the government's policy as one of 'understated response'. Theirs is a telling and an accurate phrase. Opinion in the House of Commons, roused by the national press, and in turn rousing that press, was verging on the hysterical, not least since a large number of members had, over the years, become convinced that it was the settled intention of the Foreign Office in particular, and of successive governments in general, eventually peacefully to yield up the islands to the increasingly clamorous Argentinians. As recently as December 1980 Nicholas Ridley (by 1982 a Treasury minister, but in 1980 a Foreign Office junior) had been savaged by the House because of accurate rumours that he favoured the idea of ceding sovereignty over the islands to Buenos Aires, followed by their leasing back by Britain for a lengthy period. True, Ridley had insisted that the consent of the islanders would be essential to the adoption of that plan. But a number of backbenchers – and particularly the small group which had formed the Falkland Islands Emergency Committee – simply did not believe his assurances, for they surmised that it was the intention of Foreign Office ministers and civil servants alike to use every resource of cajolery and pressure to bring the islanders around to their way of thinking.

The harrying of Nicholas Ridley by a furious House was hardly unexpected. After all, Labour ministers in both Lords and Commons – in the persons of Alun (Lord) Chalfont and Edward Rowlands – had undergone similar experiences in previous years. No minister charged with the execution of a policy designed to assuage both Argentinian ambition and island opinion could have been unaware of the fact that there was a tremendous repository of potential rage in Parliament, ready to be unleashed upon anybody who allowed it to appear that appeasement was thought to be an option in the South Atlantic. The situation was, whenever the matter came up, exacerbated by the fact that both the major parties played politics with it. Thus, Peter Shore, who had been a member of the Labour government which had considered Argentinian aspirations in a favourable light, assailed Ridley for doing exactly the same thing. And while there were very few backbenchers who had any real knowledge and understanding of the islands, there were many whose emotions were readily aroused by the few who had – those, in brief, who were organised, with great skill, in the Falkland Islands Emergency Committee, a small group whose individual members enjoyed no particular public fame, but whose simplicity and directness of purpose, based throughout on an utter refusal to do anything that might be described as handing the islanders over, commanded both respect and fervour. In the 1980 attack on Ridley, moreover, there was one compellingly authoritative voice. Julian Amery, Harold Macmillan's son-in-law, asked Ridley, in tones of a deadly if contained bitterness, whether he knew that 'for years, and here I speak with some experience, his department has wanted to get rid of this commitment?' Julian Amery is, to many middle-of-the-road politicians, a figure of fun, a dashing imperial figure out of the past, a dreamer of glories past that will none the less return. But he has a compelling presence, and a great voice. Moreover, when he spoke of his experience his listeners knew that he was speaking honestly: he had been a junior minister in the Foreign Office during the time of the Heath government. If his passion did not sway the Commons the certain knowledge that he was right, that he had seen, close up, schemes for the dissolution of the British commitment to the Falkland Islands, did.

Nicholas Ridley's unhappy experience in December 1980 – one more intense than, but in kind no different from that of other junior ministers who preceded or followed him – might have been expected by the outside chronicler to give pause to those politicians and civil servants who were engaged in what seemed to them to be the ineluctable and sensible policy of finding a method of letting the Argentinians have their way. The few who feared – or gave much attention to – the predictable outrage of Parliament at any scheme designed to achieve that end encouraged Carrington to seek the support of Prime

Minister and Cabinet alike for a public programme (of what one memorandum called the 'education of the simple') designed to win domestic support for another colonial withdrawal. Carrington ruled the idea out. It would, he thought, be too expensive; it would stir in the Prime Minister a hostile emotional reaction; and it would inflame rather than assuage hostile opinion.

Nevertheless, between 1980 and 1982 the process of emollient diplomacy continued, and President Galtieri's government engaged again and again in exchanges which they found soothing and even supportive. They had little doubt – and they were right to have little doubt – that those with whom they engaged in discourse were anxious to find a solution agreeable to Argentinian purposes. To an authoritarian government the extreme difficulty which a rebellious parliament could create for a democratic government was something quite incomprehensible and, further, over the years, nobody except Sir Maurice Oldfield – and he only in a surreptitious way – had explained to the Argentinians the impossibility of the situation in which well-disposed British politicians and diplomats found themselves. But still, knowing both the expectations that every exchange roused in Argentinian breasts, and the explosive effect that attempts to satisfy those expectations would inevitably have, the diplomatic process of trying to find a way continued.

The fact that it did dramatically summarises one of the most fundamental, and one of the most frequently repeated themes of this book. To the Foreign Office as an institution, and to Peter Carrington as an individual, the diplomatic process itself was always seen as at least equal to, and sometimes superior to the ends of policy. Dramatic diplomatic *démarches* were, no doubt, sometimes appropriate. Carrington, for example, favoured both the swift and stinging response of the Western powers to the Soviet invasion and the Western imposition of economic sanctions on the government of Poland in the wake of the curbing of the Solidarity movement led by Lech Walesa. In his judgement, however, and in that of his closest advisers, gestures, however necessary and even desirable, must not be prolonged. 'The finger of accusation,' he told one private meeting, 'cannot stay pointed for ever.' So when, after the Afghan invasion, he found himself, for the regular six-month period, chairman of the EEC's Council of foreign ministers, he proposed to make a visit to Moscow, and devised a plan that would achieve a Russian withdrawal without excessive loss of face. He found it difficult to understand that the Soviet government, entrenched at whatever cost in Asian mountains, were not in the least interested in his proposals, and his Moscow visit never took place.

Over the Falklands, both the Foreign Secretary and his department were truly caught between Scylla and Charybdis. They believed it desirable to yield up the islands, making the best deal available – and the Argentinians were lavish in their promises – for the inhabitants who wished to remain, and paying whatever was required in compensation for those who chose not to live under a foreign flag. They observed, but without anything like full emotional understanding, the mounting pressure within Argentina for a clear-cut solution. And they retired, in a state of like incomprehension, from various bruising encounters with an eternally suspicious Parliament to continue the stately minuet of talks with Latin-American opposite numbers. It would have been conceivable – if politically exceptionally difficult – to go before Parliament and the British public and argue that agreed withdrawal was necessary. It would have been possible, if not exactly agreeable to men whose whole faith lay in a belief in the essential reasonableness of their interlocuters, to tell various Argentinian spokesmen that there was nothing doing in the way of a deal. What was not, as the event was to show, possible, was to placate Parliament and Argentina at the same time. Foreign Secretary and Foreign Office sought, through patient talk, the best of both worlds. Foreign Secretary and Foreign Office got the worst of both.

In the days immediately before the invasion a cruel toll was exacted from those who had handled British policy since the election of the first Thatcher government in 1979. The whole process was speeded up: it achieved, indeed, an almost manic pace, and the contradictions of the past were made viciously manifest. Richard Luce, for example, the junior Foreign Office minister whose brief included Latin America, found himself, on Tuesday 30 March, trying to reassure the House of Commons (and, later in the day, a Conservative backbench committee) that stern measures were being taken to repel any precipitate Argentinian action and, at the same time, trying to reassure the Argentinians that it was worth their while to continue along the primrose path of diplomacy. Luce's was the dilemma that his department, and its political chiefs, had suffered for years: what was hard for him was that he had to handle a condensation of it into days, while his Foreign Secretary was preoccupied with Europe and the Middle East. He knew, though, that *Spartan* would take ten days to reach the Falklands: before that the United Kingdom would be in no position militarily to respond to, let alone repel a determined Argentinian assault. To admit openly that the submarines were, or were about to be, under way, was actually to encourage rather than discourage a pre-emptive strike.

For General Galtieri and his colleagues, of course, looked through a different window or, at least, into a different mirror. They and preceding governments of their country had been engaged in debate, that, if often tetchy, was rarely acrimonious, with British governments of different political hue for years. Hastings and Jenkins, indeed, record an Argentinian view to the effect that, over the whole period, the politics of their country had proved more stable – at least so far as the Falklands were concerned – than those of Britain. They *knew* that it had been for a long time considered a *desideratum* by the Foreign Office to end the connection with the islands. Now – again one must consider the matter as it was seen in Buenos Aires – the arcane and over-emotional reaction on the part of the House of Commons to inevitability seemed about to compel a British government which had hitherto been considered sensible to embark on a process which would make possible a military riposte to Argentinian assertion of a natural right. True, Harry Schlaudemann, the American Ambassador in Buenos Aires, told the Argentinian Foreign Minister, Nicanor Costa Mendes, on that Tuesday that Carrington had asked Alexander Haig to warn the Argentinians not to engage on an operation that might well invite massive retaliation. But the route the message had taken was too tortuous: Costa Mendes dealt with Schlaudemann through an intermediary.

It was Richard Luce's unenviable job both to reassure British politicians that measures sufficient to the hour were being taken and not to excite Argentina into pre-emption. It was insufficiently appreciated by British diplomats, though not by the representatives of the British Press in Buenos Aires, that the internal pressures on the Galtieri government were massive. *La Prensa*, the Argentinian newspaper which had won an international reputation many years previously through its opposition to an earlier Argentinian dictator, General Juan Peron, had observed, in March,[5] that 'The only thing which can save this government is a war.' It is a proposition familiar to even the most casual student of diplomatic history that authoritarian governments beset by problems at home seek diversion of discontent by adventure abroad. Thus it was with the Argentinian *junta*. And, indeed, some of the information available to them from London suggested that they would be wise to strike quickly.

It is necessary, at this point, to unravel each strand of the diplomatic skein in order to appreciate the view of the situation as seen on either side of the Atlantic, not merely, though principally, by each of the two powers mainly involved, but also by anxious outsiders, friends and allies both of Britain and Argentina. There is a great deal of disputation over when the Argentinian decision to attack became irrevocable. According to the prevailing view in the Foreign Office the decision was not taken until Friday, though ships were positioned – as, ostensibly, part of an Argentinian–Uruguyan naval exercise – some days before. In my judgement, and based on my information, the decision to attack was made on Wednesday: this, too, has been the contention of the American Central Intelligence Agency throughout the protracted and international post-mortem of the Falklands War.

I am satisfied that Italian intelligence sources informed their Argentinian counterparts, in the course of the Brussels summit, that Carrington was set on continuing with his plan for a visit to Israel. The Argentinians, naturally, understood this to mean that the Foreign Secretary did not, as Nicanor Costa Mendes was already reasonably sure he did not, consider events in the South Atlantic to be of an importance comparable with those in Brussels and Tel Aviv. I am satisfied, further, that although all the necessary evidence of Argentinian intention was available – in the form of signals between Brussels, Rome and Buenos Aires – at the meeting of the Joint Intelligence Committee on Wednesday, it was not properly understood. That is to say that most of it was what is called 'raw' intelligence – cuttings of news stories, copies of editorials like that already referred to in *La Prensa*, transcripts of voluble conversations between Rome and

5. *La Prensa* has a notable record of independent criticism of various Argentinian dictatorships.

Buenos Aires – and the JIC normally waits for 'processed' intelligence, that is, considered and neat analysis of what has come in.

On the evidence and indications available to them, therefore, the Argentinian government drew perfectly reasonable conclusions. A landing in force on the islands would, they believed, be only nominally opposed. It would be followed by intense and outraged British protests at the United Nations, in Washington, and in European and other capitals. What they did not anticipate was that something like the plan devised by Henry Leach and his staff on the Monday afternoon would receive a ready, indeed an enthusiastic and fervent acceptance by the British government.

Israeli politicians are less inclined to respect for the formal niceties of diplomatic intercourse than are the representatives of other countries, particularly the British. Carrington's Israeli hosts, therefore, resentful as they were at what they took to be unwarranted interference in the affairs of their region, set about baiting him immediately upon his arrival in Tel Aviv. Their none-too-subtle remarks to the effect that he would be better employed in London, preparing whatever riposte he considered suitable to an imminent Argentinian attack, were (it is said humorously) brushed aside by him as a cover for Israeli unwillingness to talk Middle Eastern politics. The Israelis were not exactly unhappy when, during dinner, he received a summons to return home at once. It was not clear yet whether General Menendez had landed; but it was certain that he was about to.

The Prime Minister hastily convened an emergency meeting of the Cabinet for Thursday evening. 'We were all in a state of shock,' said one minister present. 'All except her. She was just hopping mad with everybody, the Argies and even us, including Peter and John.' Already the network of British diplomacy was at full stretch, seeking last-minute intervention by the United States, by the European powers, by any country, in short, that was deemed to have the slightest influence in Buenos Aires. It was clear from press, constituency, parliamentary party and opposition sentiment that – again in the words of one of those present – 'something definite would have to be done. Maybe even something drastic.' It was already accepted that the House of Commons would have to meet on Saturday – the first such meeting since the Egyptian annexation of the Suez Canal in 1956 – for the situation was not expected to be totally clear by the end of Friday's business. The waters were, moreover, somewhat muddied by Foreign Office and Joint Intelligence Committee assessments to the effect that even at this late hour Argentina would stay her hand, or engage only in incursions designed to have a symbolic effect, such as the earlier landings on South Georgia. In putting forward these assessments – which the Prime Minister had already seen on Wednesday – Carrington was, of course, grasping at straws, and he knew it. However, his natural desire to hope for the best was reinforced by his relative ignorance of the latest fast-moving events. He had arrived from Israel that evening, and had not been party to earlier exchanges between the Prime Minister and other ministers, as well as between civil servants and the First Sea Lord. He was still trying to get his bearings, and he was horrified when, after a certain amount of more or less desultory and worried discussion, the Prime Minister intervened to say, 'Gentlemen, we shall have to fight.' 'The woman's gone mad', a horrified Carrington exclaimed as the meeting broke up. 'It won't, it can't come to that.'

The first bricks in the edifice of a military response were, however, already in place. It was fairly quickly appreciated, by colleagues and opponents alike, that it was very much in the Prime Minister's nature to leap for the most decisive option. Indeed, it was commonly agreed at Westminster over the coming weeks that no other Prime Minister would have so readily taken the decision to use force. But Mrs Thatcher did have one practical advantage: she had talked to Henry Leach, and had been convinced by his arguments.

Sir Henry had arrived at her room in the House of Commons on Wednesday evening to find a meeting already convened to discuss the situation in the South Atlantic. Only two Cabinet members – Humphrey Atkins, by then Carrington's spokesman in the House of Commons, and John Nott – were present. The First Sea Lord's contribution to debate was decisive. He explained at great length what had already been done: the submarines were, or would shortly be, on their way; the Fleet had been alerted; various land commanders had been quietly warned to prepare themselves for action. Interestingly, neither he nor any other of the government's chief service advisers had been asked to attend this meeting: he had set out for the House of Commons only when he had discovered that his minister was there and it was some time, indeed, before Mrs Thatcher realised that he was available. Once present, however, he came exceptionally well out of the kind of ruthless cross-examination to which she frequently subjects ministers. He stressed, in particular, the need for a balanced – in other words, a mighty – fleet and – music to her ears – confirmed that its first elements could put to sea by the weekend. By Wednesday evening, therefore, the Prime Minister had the elements of a policy to present to the House. By Thursday evening it was unlikely that any of her Cabinet colleagues – and there were some with deep reservations about the wisdom of the course on which she was about to embark – could have deflected her.

Her decisiveness did not, however, suffice to restore order to a badly shaken government, or to a badly shaken Foreign Office. Leach's intervention, according to another Cabinet member, 'had put the spine back into John Nott'. But, although Friday saw the smooth convening of the inter-service committees necessary to set the machinery of war in motion, confusion still marked the activities of the politicians. 'After all,' said one of them defensively, 'we didn't even know that the Argies *had* landed, and the FO had asked Reagan to intervene with Galtieri personally. We set a lot of store by that; we thought that the Americans had much greater clout in Argentina than they in fact did.' President Reagan, after a four-hour wait, did manage to get General Galtieri to come to the telephone: but he was totally unsuccessful in his attempt to persuade the chairman of the *junta* to alter his plans. Even so, the British politicians, and particularly the ministers at the Foreign Office, went on hoping against hope, even in the face of irrefutable evidence. 'But don't you see,' said one diplomat to whom I put this point, 'that is what we're *for*. We had to go on hoping.'

Going on hoping had consequences that were embarrassing, and might even have been disastrous. The Argentinians landed at dawn on Friday, 2 April. The emergency Cabinet meeting that morning reckoned, however, that information to this effect was insufficiently conclusive and, after hurried consultation, Carrington allowed Atkins to make a statement in the House of Commons to this effect. He went so far, indeed, as to deny that an invasion had taken place.

Hours later a contrite and shaken Atkins, and a Foreign Secretary who was clearly shaken – if not yet contrite – had to retract that denial. The Ministry of Defence announced that a Task Force was being

assembled for service in the South Atlantic. The Leader of the House –
John Biffen, who was believed to be very nearly as unenthusiastic
about the Prime Minister's declaration of Thursday evening as was
Carrington – got in touch with the business managers of the other
parties. In due course the government announced that the House of
Commons would meet on Saturday morning.

Being a member of the House of Lords Carrington was spared the
ordeal of facing a House of Commons in full cry. So was Atkins and,
for that matter, Richard Luce, the junior Foreign Office minister in the
Commons, for the Prime Minister opened the debate on the government side, and it was closed by the hapless Secretary of State for
Defence, John Nott. Most public, and certainly most Conservative
opinion held the two Secretaries of State, and their departments, guilty
of failing to predict, and then to prevent, the Argentinian incursion.
The government's conduct so far had but a solitary committed Conservative backbench defender, Ray Whitney: the fact that Whitney
had been a member of the Diplomatic Service was sufficient, in the
mood of the moment, to condemn his plea for an understanding of the
Argentinian position and a negotiated settlement. The main opposition parties had a field day. It was not just that they had facing them a
Conservative government strung tight on the rack of a foreign policy
blunder, when foreign policy was widely supposed to be a Tory *forte*.
As was demonstrated in the Saturday debate by Dr David Owen –
subsequently supported by James Callaghan, the former Labour
Prime Minister – a Labour government of 1977, in which Owen had
been Foreign Secretary, had prevented an Argentinian attack by the
quiet deployment of a relatively modest naval force. The Thatcher
government – so the opposition argument ran – by calling out of
service the Antarctic supply ship HMS *Endurance* had given the
go-ahead to General Galtieri and his adventurous colleagues. True,
the guns of *Endurance* were vastly inferior to the armament that could
be deployed by the Argentinian navy, and a token garrison of Royal
Marines *did* remain on the islands. But the announcement of the
scrapping of *Endurance*, whose captain – though this was not known
at the time – had consistently warned of the imminence of invasion,
the limp-wristed attitude of British diplomats during bilateral discussions on the future, and the widely held belief that it had for a long time
been Foreign Office policy to hand the islands over to Argentina and

re-settle the islanders, all convinced a majority of MPs that crucial errors of will and judgement had already been made. Nott was reduced to railing at the opposition, asserting the general superiority of Conservative defence policy, and roundly asserting determination for the future. His speech won little support and no sympathy.

But the intervention that was most telling, in so far as it had an immediate – and, according to one of her staff, devastating – impact on the Prime Minister herself, was that of Enoch Powell. Now the Official Ulster Unionist member for Down South, and a man who has almost as a matter of habit created havoc in Conservative ranks over the years, Powell is still regarded by some as the conscience of the Tory Party. Those who regard him as such include a disproportionate number of Mrs Thatcher's closest adherents. She herself refers to him as 'golden-hearted Enoch', and regrets deeply the finicky and quirky conscience that required him to take his departure from the party ranks. Like many on that Saturday morning, Powell doubted whether, in spite of all that had been said from the government front bench, the Cabinet would have the resolution to meet force with force. In measured tones of irony and scepticism, he referred to the Prime Minister's known liking for the soubriquet 'Iron Lady' – first bestowed on her by Marjorie Proops of the *Daily Mirror*, but later taken up by *Red Star*, the Soviet Army Journal – and predicted that coming weeks 'will show of what metal she is made'. The pun was vintage Powell. The remark struck home.

By Saturday evening the government was on the ropes, but not yet down. From Wednesday onwards contradictory instructions had flowed from London to various elements of the armed forces. The instructions – varying at extremes between alert and stand down – were confused for several reasons. Nobody knew whether the government would, in the end, have the resolution to fight at a range of 8,000 miles. Nobody knew what size and type of force would form the most effective adjunct to the diplomatic efforts the American government were about to launch. Nobody, in short, knew anything very much about anything.

However, by Sunday it was apparent that there was a substantial majority both in the party and the country for action. It was also apparent to members of her government that the Prime Minister was now not merely determined on action if it were necessary, but actually preferred it to diplomacy. By Monday Carrington had decided to resign. Atkins, Luce and Nott all decided to go with him. The Prime Minister's own blandishments and urgings had no effect on the decision of the Foreign Office team. Nott, however, responded to her blunter refusal of his submission, though he was, at the end of the war, to announce his retirement from politics altogether.

Neither the international diplomacy which proceeded at an increasingly frenetic pace as the Task Force sailed south nor the fighting that immediately succeeded its arrival in the South Atlantic are a part of this book. However, the fact that a somewhat incredulous world – and an almost as incredulous Westminster – increasingly accepted over this weekend that Mrs Thatcher was willing to go to war, does seem to have played a major part in Carrington's decision to leave office. Given, moreover, that the eventual outcome of the fighting was to place the Prime Minister on a pinnacle of authority within her party, and in the country, which no Conservative Leader had enjoyed for many years, her attitude and his over the period from Thursday to Monday are of considerable interest to any student of modern British politics. The difference in reaction and decision between the two of them highlights what seems to me to be the nature of the most important debate about the character of British politics that has occurred since the last war.

'Well,' said Carrington on television on the Monday night, 'what we got wrong was that the Argentinians invaded . . .' Though it was evident in this particularly arduous interview with Robert Kee that the now former Foreign Secretary was under considerable strain, he preserved a great deal of that debonair aplomb which had become, over the years, so integral a part of his public image. The Prime Minister's supporters – and at least two of her personal staff – were deeply offended by that shrug with which he accompanied his explanation of how it had come about that his department's prediction of Argentinian intentions had been so manifestly wrong. There were, he said simply, divisions of opinion, '. . . the assessments were different'. They were even more offended when newspaper reports of his pre-recorded conversation with Kee appeared and Carrington was quoted on the sheer relief of being out of office, 'I can stick my tongue out at you now if I like.' This kind of languid frivolity does not represent the sort of style favoured in the Prime Minister's circle. Nor, for that matter, was it appropriate to the temper of the country or the pressure of the hour.

While it would be true to say that a great many people – whose views were accurately summarised in a particularly stinging and mordant article by Andrew Alexander in the *Daily Mail* – thought that Carrington should resign, the number who believed he actually would was far smaller. He had not, after all – said his critics – resigned over the Crichel Down affair[6] nor over the Vassal scandal.[7] He had remained remarkably unshaken in his confidence in his own political judgement after his strenuously urged advice to Edward Heath in 1974 had led to electoral defeat and the deposition of Heath as Leader of the Conservative Party. His love for his job was well known. His friends wanted him to remain at his post, and his enemies feared that he would do so.

The Prime Minister tried hard throughout Monday, 5 April 1982 to prevent the resignation of the Foreign Office ministers. It was thus supposed, given that part of her letter to Carrington on his resignation was personally flattering, that she saw his loss to her Cabinet as a severe, perhaps even a body, blow.

Almost every Prime Minister for a generation – and a large number of Foreign Secretaries – has, at one time or another, come to distrust the Foreign Office as an institution, a remarkable phenomenon discussed in Chapter 6. But Mrs Thatcher had more reasons, large and small, than most.

There was, first, hers and their attitude to relations with Soviet Russia. When she won the leadership of the Party she was as acutely aware as her critics of her lack of experience. It is generally assumed that a British Prime Minister – and perhaps especially a Conservative one – will have had wide experience of high office before reaching No 10 Downing Street. Even Stanley Baldwin, in the early 1920s, whose rise to power was extraordinarily fast, had been, however briefly, Chancellor of the Exchequer. Mrs Thatcher had merely been Secretary of State for Education and Science, and a remarkably controversial one at that. And she had, of course, absolutely no foreign policy record.

6. Below, p. 54ff.
7. Below, p. 66ff.

She did, however, have very strong views, largely developed with the help of some of her closer friends and advisers who, though essentially concerned with the development of her distinctive domestic economic policies, tended almost invariably to be hawkish on the USSR and lukewarm about Britain's commitment to the European Economic Community. Thus, in 1976, the Leader embarked on the series of speeches which earned her the title of 'Iron Lady'. She revelled in it. The Foreign Office shuddered.

She gave particular offence in July 1976 when, without seeking an FO briefing – which is available as a matter of courtesy to senior opposition politicians – and without even consulting the Conservative Research Department (she had good reason to know that the Shadow Foreign Secretary, Reginald Maudling, opposed her line) she made a speech ferociously attacking the Eastern bloc in general and the Soviet Union in particular. Moreover, she chose as the occasion for her speech the first anniversary of the Helsinki Declaration, the corner-stone of that policy of East-West détente so much treasured by both the Foreign Office and the American State Department. An FO observer of the speech – present unofficially simply because he lived near Dorking, where it was delivered – said to me afterwards over a drink, 'I think your woman's gone crazy. Please God she'll never be Prime Minister.'

Again, during the 1975 referendum on whether or not Britain would remain a member of the EEC – undertaken by the Wilson government in fulfilment of an election promise – Mrs Thatcher took a back seat, leaving Edward Heath to lead the Tory campaign to stay in the EEC. Though this act of self-abnegation was principally a recognition of Heath's pre-eminence as a pro-EEC campaigner, and though she did make some contribution to winning the vote for continued membership, it was widely believed, both among Heath's still substantial number of supporters and in the Foreign Office itself, that her reticence masked reluctance.

Mutual suspicion revived when she became Prime Minister and embarked on a series of first-class rows with continental governments on the issue of Britain's contributions to the Community budget. From the moment of his appointment as Foreign Secretary Carrington had thrown himself into the European part of his world rôle, to the immense gratification of his staff. While he accepted that some reduction in the British contribution to the budget was highly desirable from a domestic political point of view, the vehemence of the Prime Minister, and her insistence on exacting massive sums – an insistence backed by the scarcely veiled threat of disrupting the Community if she did not get her way – appalled him. Again and again the Prime Minister played for higher stakes. Again and again the Foreign Secretary strove to soften her line. And again and again the Foreign Office leaked stories to the Press that she had backed down. The fact that she eventually won the surcease she sought, if only for a limited period, reinforced her doubts about the perspicacity of the British Diplomatic Service.

All this was part of the background to the uneasy climate which existed between Downing Street and the Foreign Office – and which continues to exist. It was frequently smoothed over by Carrington's adroit diplomacy, but it continued to smoulder, and it was the cause of the fact that, in Mrs Thatcher's letter to John Nott refusing his resignation, she stressed that blame for the fiasco did not attach to the Ministry of Defence, but to another department.

At the very least blame should be shared for, if the FO had been culpably blind in not reading correctly the political signals of a bellicose character emanating from Buenos Aires, then the Secretary of State for Defence could be said to have been a trifle careless in considering the military requirements of the Falkland Islands. Shortly after his departure, when a rumour circulated to the effect that the Foreign Office had prevented the Ministry of Defence from sending a submarine to the islands before the invasion (or at the very least had failed to support their desire to do so) Carrington wrote briefly, but in cold anger, to *The Times* to deny it, and implicitly invited Nott to deny it as well. Nott has so far not done so.

Again, on often quite small issues, the Prime Minister has found herself – as her staff at least believe – frustrated by the Foreign Office. To take but one example, her then Political Secretary, Richard Ryder, discovered by accident in 1980 that Mrs Raoul Wallenberg, wife of the distinguished Swedish diplomat who had done so much to rescue so many Jews from the clutches of the Nazis during the war, who had been arrested by the Russians, and who is believed by many to be still alive in captivity, had written to the Prime Minister seeking her intercession but had received, even after a long interval, no reply.

What puzzled the Wallenberg family about the delay was that it was in such seeming contradiction to Mrs Thatcher's known and proclaimed views about human rights, especially when those who suffered were the victims of Soviet oppression. Investigation revealed that, after its arrival at Downing Street, the letter had, in the ordinary course of business, been sent to the Foreign Office for their remarks and a draft reply, and it had lain there untended for some time. To the rebuke that descended on their head the FO staff pointed to the vast volume of paper they had to deal with every day. To that, of course, the reply was that any intelligent appreciation of the Prime Minister's character and record would have shown that this was a missive which should have been dealt with as a matter of priority. To this day the suspicion remains at No 10 that the Foreign Office was as usual dilatory about and indifferent to Mrs Thatcher's susceptibilities and interests, inclined to dismiss as amateurish or emotional an interest in the fate of a long-vanished and, quite possibly, dead diplomat.

On the other hand, in another human rights case – that concerning the boat people fleeing from the delights of Communist rule in Vietnam – it was Mrs Thatcher who first reacted with a firm negative to the proposal that some of them be given refuge in this country, and Carrington, after visiting a refugee camp in Hong Kong, who persuaded her to change her mind. Even his friends were astonished by the strength of his reaction to what he saw in Hong Kong, for he is a man who, though prone to sharp outbursts of temper (and criticised as impatient even by his wife), has always schooled himself to avoid the appearance of emotion, and conceals his feelings under the cloak of his humour.

'Resignation,' Enoch Powell once observed, 'on a matter of principle or because of a recognition of incompetence, has gone out of fashion in British politics.' Certainly, as Edward Heath likes to stress, there were no major resignations from his government on these grounds, the departure of the Home Secretary, Reginald Maudling, having occurred because of his sensitivity to police investigation of the financial affairs of some business associates. The only resignation on grounds of principle from either of the last two Conservative governments was that of Teddy Taylor in 1972, because of his opposition to British membership of the EEC. The press and the political world were alike taken aback, therefore, when both Atkins and Luce resigned with

Carrington. It was certainly the case, as Carrington believed, that their departure made it easier for the Prime Minister to pursue a more single-minded policy in the weeks that followed, and to shrug off accusations to the effect that she had been as remiss as her former Foreign Secretary in predicting Argentinian actions. But the fall of Carrington symbolised an indictment by events not just of three men, but of a whole attitude to foreign policy and diplomacy, and of a whole historical tradition of its conduct.

3. THE PEER

We see yonder the beginning of day,
But I think we shall never see the end of it . . .
I am afraid there are few die well that die in a battle.

William Shakespeare, *Henry V.*

Peter Carrington had an enviably happy and assured childhood. He was, say contemporaries, a sunny boy at Eton, and has preserved no memories of pain or unhappiness from his time at that academy. It was not, he says, until he arrived at Sandhurst – he had early formed the ambition to be a soldier, though he can now recall no specific reason for it – that he realised that life could be unpleasant, where 'you were done over a bit'. In his first term, particularly, he had a singularly unpleasant time, and has recorded that it took him three months to find all the pieces of his rifle after a senior cadet had dismantled it into its 179 parts and tossed them all through a window. The college authorities, whose policy it was not to interfere with the ragging activities of students, were of no comfort to him; his natural shyness inhibited self-assertion; and his lack of interest in the hardier, sporting sides of Sandhurst life left him as something of a man apart. 'He was perfectly well-liked,' said a contemporary, 'and he worked jolly hard. But he did it in a quiet way and one never expected him to be a star or anything like that. There was always a sort of reserve about him, a kind of remoteness, if you like. He could flare up – he has a very quick temper – but he didn't do it often. I always thought he had the makings of a really good regular officer, but I would have thought that he was born too late to reach the top. He would have been perfect in the old days of the Indian Empire.'

The security – financial, at any rate – in Carrington's life came from notably imaginative eighteenth-century achievements. His ancestor Thomas Smith set up the first provincial bank in England, in Nottingham. His son, Robert, transferred it to London, and it is he whom Carrington usually mentions when he refers, with pride, to the family's banking traditions. He made, for example, lengthy and snappish reference to that tradition when, in 1967, it was suggested that his appointment as chairman of the Australia-New Zealand Bank was due solely to his peerage, and to the fact that he had had a stint as British High Commissioner in Australia.

Of the Carrington ancestors it is Robert and Charles – the third baron – who stand out by reason both of achievement and individuality. Robert, having settled in somewhat palatial circumstances in London – he found it possible to endow his eight daughters with £20,000 each, without any marked dimunition of the contents of his coffers – was bold enough, and confident enough, to take on the rôle of banker and personal adviser to William Pitt the Younger. Pitt was unquestionably a great Prime Minister and – with a certain amount of help from Smith – a prudent guardian of the nation's financial affairs. He ended a period of rampant inflation. He established the Sinking Fund. He made it possible, by astute stewardship, for the country to meet the horrendous cost of the wars with revolutionary and Napoleonic France. His personal financial affairs, on the other hand, were always in an embarrassing state: when they were not embarrassing they were disastrous, and they were frequently ruinous. Nor did even the canny Mr Smith manage to pound sense into his wayward friend's head, though he frequently rescued Pitt from the brink with loans that he must have known would never be repaid.

In the eighteenth as in other centuries friendship with the great in public life is expected to lead to honours and preferment: it may even be cultivated for that reason. Honours as such, however, were not what the redoubtable Robert Smith sought. He merely asked that he be allowed to use Horse Guards as a passage of convenience between his Whitehall home and various places of business. Permission to do this being refused by King George III, Pitt provided his friend with solace in the form of an Irish barony in 1796, the King, who disliked those in trade, including bankers, holding out for a year before agreeing to the up-grading of the title, converting it into an English one which carried with it a seat in the House of Lords. In 1839 Robert's son changed the family surname to accord with the title, though there is the slight oddity that the family name is spelt with one 'r' and the name of the peerage with two. 'I don't know why that should be,' said the present Lord Carrington, 'perhaps the old boy was drunk when he signed whatever it was he had to sign.'

Robert Smith for some time sat in the House of Commons as member for a Nottinghamshire seat, but it was his descendant Charles, the third baron, who went furthest in politics. By this time the Carringtons had become Liberals. (When the suggestion was made to Peter Carrington that he secretly held to those views on economic and social policies which Mrs Thatcher designates 'wet' and whose proponents describe as 'Disraelian', a neat remark turned the point aside. 'Oh, not Disraelian,' he said. 'My family spent ages fighting him, you know.') Charles became a close friend of Edward VIII when that monarch was Prince of Wales, and was thus a colourful habitué of Edward's fun-loving set. Partly, it is believed, because of the Prince's intervention on his behalf he was appointed to an Australian governorship, thus beginning a connection between the family and that continent (Peter's father was at school there for a time) which continues into the present. Apart from his tour of duty as High Commissioner there, and his chairmanship of the Australia-New Zealand Bank, Peter Carrington has more than once, but particularly in the second half of the 1960s, when he was having an exceptionally difficult time as Leader of the House of Lords, been proposed as Australia's Governor-General. Partly because of his competent execution of his antipodean duties Charles Carrington, after the landslide Liberal general election victory of 1906, entered government as Sir Henry Campbell-Bannerman's Minister of Agriculture. The Liberal Party having been ruined by its own factional divisions and the contemporary rise of Labour having occurred, the family drifted back to its Conservative home in the 1920s.

Two events, occurring within a year of each other, changed Carrington's tranquil life and disrupted the orderly path on which he had set his feet. The first was the death of his father, in 1938, when he was only nineteen. The second was the outbreak of the Second World War.

The family estate, in the Chilterns, consists of about a thousand acres, its centre being a 300-year-old manor house. Substantial investment adds to the income derived from what has always been a well-managed estate and has, under its present owner, become a remarkably profitable and efficient one, especially renowned for its bulls and bees – for Carrington is notably interested in the manufacture of honey. Well-established in wealth and status though the family was in 1938, the precipitate assumption of his heritage and his title was, quite apart from his natural grief, a potentially unmanning experience for a youngster. 'I suddenly found myself,' he once recalled, 'a real lord rather than a pretend one. And it didn't help at all in the Army, at my age.' Evidently, sooner or later, a choice would have to be made between heritage and military service.

In 1938, however, the European political situation was such that no patriotic and ambitious young man would be likely to abandon a secure, if lowly rung in the armed services. Carrington stayed where he was, in the Grenadier Guards. The war that had been so long feared, but by so few expected, came the following year.

'I was damn sure,' said a brother-officer who served with Carrington through a war that was from the personal point of view quiet until almost its end, 'he was going to be the toffee-nosed silver spoon type. You know, all languid and full of jokes. But he was a very good officer indeed, kept exactly the right distance from his men, but was always ready to listen to people's problems, and to help when he could. He was brave, too, I never saw him scared. He more than deserved his Military Cross.'

Carrington won his MC for bravery under fire during the Allied advance through Belgium in 1945. He was now a Major, and his unit was subjected to intense fire from German tanks seeking to break through the encroaching allied lines. Carrington is not given to reminiscence about his military exploits, and usually deflects enquiries with humour. Once, in January 1964, when, in addition to his duties as Leader of the House of Lords, he had assumed a number of quasi-ministerial duties connected principally with foreign policy, he was in Brussels to attend a meeting of GATT (General Agreement on Tariffs and Trade) nations. His Belgian hosts, learning that he had fought in their country, politely suggested that he might make reference to that fact in the course of an after-dinner speech. He did so, but in his own way.

He had, Carrington told his audience, but two regrets over his sojourn in Belgium. He had been present at the liberation of Brussels, and had liberated the entire stock of wines laid aside for the delectation of the German High Command. His first regret was that conscience required him to share the plunder with Belgian officers. His second was that, although champagne had been one of his favourite drinks at that time, the depredations he had helped inflict on the stores he had found had entirely destroyed his taste for the drink, and he had never touched it since. This, as a matter of interest, was true. Later in the year, when he had helped conclude a deal on behalf not only of his own country, but of the North Atlantic Treaty Organisation as a whole, with the recalcitrant Dom Mintoff, Prime Minister of Malta, he joined in the celebrations which invariably accompany the conclusion of tortuous and protracted negotiations. The Maltese Prime Minister raised a glass of champagne to the health of the British negotiator, but Carrington replied in port. The *New Statesman* magazine contrived to see this action as some kind of subtle insult to Mintoff. But his wife later confirmed that he had not drunk champagne since the war, not even at the twenty-first birthday parties of their children, nor at the marriage of their elder daughter. He cannot have had it altogether socially easy during the life of the government headed by Edward Heath when, according to Douglas Hurd, then Heath's Political Secretary and now Secretary of State for Northern Ireland, the quaffing of champagne – '*the* political drink' – in large quantities was virtually *de rigueur*.[1]

The end of the war found young Major the Lord Carrington in a very different position, and in quite a different state of mind, from its beginning. He had married, in 1942, a beautiful Scotswoman, Iona McClean. They had hesitated for some time before taking the plunge, as did many other young couples at the time (though numbers, of course, married in haste to repent at leisure) for fear that she would be left a widow. Now, in 1945, with the country entering the painful throes of reconstruction, Carrington found himself a family man, engaged in the process of rethinking the objectives of his own life as well.

He decided to leave the army, and devote himself to family, business and politics. Like others of the officer class who rose to prominence in the Conservative party in the 1960s and 1970s – William Whitelaw is an outstanding example – Carrington had acquired an acute social conscience in the armed forces. The necessity of attending to the needs, hopes and worries of his men and, more particularly, the painful duty of writing to the kin of men wounded or killed, had given him

1. Hurd, *op. cit.*, p. 71.

knowledge and understanding of the lives of others far less fortunate than himself. This accretion of fact and impulse he was now determined to put to public use. Unlike others who developed the same feelings during the war and decided that those feelings required a political outlet – Major William Whitelaw, Major Iain Macleod, Pilot Officer Anthony Barber and (though the direction of his ambition was rather different) Brigadier J. Enoch Powell, come to mind – Carrington was not required to engage in the time-consuming business of seeking a parliamentary nomination. He simply took his father's seat in the House of Lords. He was still only twenty-six years of age.

It is important for the contemporary reader to remember how formative an experience the war was for the generation of political leaders – especially in the Conservative Party – that is now passing. As a young girl the present Prime Minister had the experience of providing junior help in service canteens in Oxford: no conceivable successor to her will have any more than childhood memories of the great war against Nazi Germany, while the present Leader of the Opposition was, of course, practically a baby when peace came. It is difficult, therefore, for today's students and followers of politics to appreciate how the war marked men and women and how deep assumptions, often barely understood, affected the attitudes to public life and to the business of making decisions in government of the political generation which had its last fling in the Conservative leadership election of 1975. Margaret Thatcher won that contest. Of her opponents Edward Heath, Hugh Fraser, William Whitelaw and John Peyton had all served in the war, and Peyton had been a prisoner. Since, of the remaining two candidates, James Prior had served in the army in India and Germany in 1946, only the victor and Sir Geoffrey Howe had no military experience at all. It may be that Mrs Thatcher's successor will have done national service, and, of course, there have been in her Cabinets men who saw action between 1939 and 1945, but those who had personal formative experiences similar to those which shaped Peter Carrington are passing on from British public life.

The instinct towards ameliorative social legislation – what might be called an instinctive, an emotional feeling of support for Welfare State politics – was an almost invariable characteristic of the wartime generation of Tory politicians. Other young men and women, of course, took their instincts further, and joined the Labour Party, or political groupings much further to the left. As the war moved to its close, further, the various services' educational corps were almost entirely staffed by those who favoured left-wing politics and this, combined with memories of the depression of the 1930s, was an important factor in the plurality that Labour enjoyed in 1945 among those voters still in uniform.

The turmoil of the closing months of the war, and of the immediate post-war period, produced other effects on Carrington than those associated with the general urge to assume a public duty. Many men and women came out of the war with a deep respect for the military endeavours of the Soviet Union, and a consequent sympathy for the social doctrines in which the public ideology of that country was encapsulated. Carrington's observation of educational trends in the armed services, and his own analysis of Soviet power and intentions, produced in him an opposite effect. When even Conservative politicians were expressing a warm regard for the gallantry of Russia Carrington viewed her advance in Eastern and Central Europe with alarm. Communism he regarded with a deeper horror than even his Tory contemporaries, who tended to dismiss hard left-wing ideology with the casual contempt they felt it deserved. To this day he has a general dislike of any political creed that may be called an ideology, saying of his own party in 1973, 'I never think that the Conservative Party is at its most attractive or most interesting or most useful when it is trying, out of character, to be ideological.' Such expressions of opinion have naturally encouraged observers to place him on the so-called 'wet' wing of Tory politics, and not unfairly, scrupulously though he has in recent years refrained from intervention in domestic affairs. For left-wing ideology at home, however, he has a loathing that masks a kind of fear and it is not, I believe, fanciful to ascribe the furious determination with which, in 1973 and 1974, he argued for a general election in the face of the coal miners' strike, to attitudes that were developed, and even honed, by 1945.

In 1946, in any event, a new age had begun. Carrington took his part in it through his family, his estate and his seat in the Lords. He also became a management trainee at de Havillands, thus maintaining a connection with defence matters which, with only a couple of interruptions, has lasted to this day, when he occupies the chair of the Secretary-General of NATO.

From the beginning Carrington was an assiduous and eager junior politician in the Lords, making it clear to his superiors that he was no dilettante youngster, nor even the kind of hereditary peer who, though conscientious, concentrated on a limited range of subjects of special interest to himself. 'He was very quick,' said an exact contemporary in the Upper House, who had himself unexpectedly succeeded to his title at an early age. 'I don't mean that he was intellectual, and he often seemed to make no effort at all. But he *was* charming and amusing, and he could get up a subject very quickly, or at least at short notice make a speech which set out the general principles of a subject in the most down-to-earth and commonsense sort of way. I think we all liked him.' This liking resulted in Carrington becoming a junior Lords Whip in 1947.

The House of Lords being very unlike the House of Commons in its conduct of procedure and personal relations, it is virtually impossible for the disciplinarian qualities that can make a man a good whip in the Lower House to be acceptable in the Upper. It was Carrington's grace that got him his first government appointment, and, perhaps, his willingness to undertake tasks that often seemed thankless. He could listen, and he could persuade: these were the requisite talents for a Lords' Whip, talents which were to serve him more than well when he became Leader of that House.

Between the shattering general election defeat of 1945 and the return to power – still under Churchill's leadership – in 1951, the Conservative Party underwent a painful process of revision, one usually associated with the work of R. A. Butler and the Conservative Research Department, among the post-war luminaries on the staff of which were Iain Macleod, Reginald Maudling and Enoch Powell. The details of the reconstruction of the party's policy and of its image need not concern us here and have, in any event, already been written about at length.[2] Suffice it to say that the efforts masterminded by Butler, which issued in a long series of policy documents which commanded a great deal of attention, resulted in the party presenting to the electorate in 1950 (when the battle was narrowly lost) and in 1951 a new vision of Conservatism. All the main structural changes enacted by the Attlee government, particularly those concerned with provision for

2. See R. A. Butler, *The Art of the Possible* (London, 1971).

health and social security, but including the nationalisation of key sectors of the economy, were accepted by the Opposition as, from then, permanent features of the structure of British society. There would be tinkering, certainly; the irritating controls imposed on individual economic conduct would be abolished; and the steel industry would, probably, be de-nationalised[3] but the main outlines of the post-war settlement imposed, following their triumphal endorsement by the electorate in 1945, by Attlee and his colleagues would remain in place. Henceforth, the Conservative Party when in government would rule according to the rules of, and within a framework designed by, the Labour Party. It was not until 1979 that this consensus was challenged, and even by 1985 those who made the challenge, led by Margaret Thatcher, have not overturned it.

The Attlee reforms were a vital part of the background of the young Carrington's induction into politics. The social and even most of the economic reforms introduced were agreeable enough to him, for reasons outlined above. In one particular area, however, and particularly after he became an Opposition Whip in 1947, plans were afoot which engaged his full attention, and his reactions to which and understanding of which constituted a vital part of his political training. It is not too much, indeed, to say that Carrington's experiences as a Whip and a peer on the opposition benches between 1947 and 1951 played a critical part in his conduct of high policy as Leader of the House of Lords between 1963 and 1970. The doctrines with regard to the proper behaviour of the Upper House during the first two Wilson administrations (1964–6 and 1966–70), and the tactics which he used in day-to-day controversy, all proceed from the period of his blooding in politics.

The tactical situation in which both government and opposition found themselves after 1945 was, on the face of it, simple. Labour enjoyed a massive majority in the House of Commons, of 146 over all opposition and 180 over the Conservatives alone. The Conservatives enjoyed a majority in the Lords of a roughly equal magnitude, though one not possible to calculate exactly, because of the greater independence of party whips of the peerage. The powers of the House of Lords were governed, broadly, by the Act of 1911, imposed upon it by a

3. See Richard Rose, *The problem of party government* (London, 1974). p. 74f.

Liberal government backed by the willingness of King George V to create a sufficient number of Liberal peers to pass any legislation that the Prime Minister, Asquith, desired in order to curb the opposition of the Lords to him. The 1911 Act removed the power of the Lords to reject what were called 'Money Bills', essentially those arising from the Budget, or involving government expenditure. The Act further restricted the power of the Lords to reject or amend other government legislation; an ordinary Bill would become law, whatever the Upper House wanted, if it passed the Commons in three successive sessions, provided only that two years had passed between Second Commons Reading (the debate on the principle of a Bill) and its final passage by that House. Roughly, therefore, the Lords could hold up a government Bill for two years, during which time, of course, anything could happen.

Between the wars there were numerous proposals for a more fundamental – and, if possible, agreed – reform of the Lords, and the likelihood that some of its members should be elected was more than once mooted. By 1945, however, nothing material had been done. The immediate and dramatic question arose: what would be the attitude of a Conservative House of Lords to the radical reforming programme of a Labour House of Commons, a programme which most certainly overthrew many of the assumptions on the right conduct of the affairs of the nation clung to by Tory peers? Into this maelstrom the politically inexperienced Carrington was thrown.

The position of the Prime Minister, Clement Attlee, was clear. Unlike some politicians on the fringe of the Labour Party, he had no desire whatsoever to abolish the hereditary peerage, nor the House of Lords itself. Indeed when, in 1950, the present Lord Hailsham, then, as Quintin Hogg, a Conservative Commons backbencher, asked for – demanded, would perhaps be a better word – legislation allowing him to disclaim the peerage he had just inherited from his father, Attlee turned him down flat. On the other hand the Prime Minister had pledged himself – and Attlee never took pledges lightly – to ensure that the Lords would not be allowed to frustrate or scotch the reformist proposals contained in his 1945 manifesto.[4]

The cooler heads in both Conservative and Labour leaderships

4. Kenneth Harris, *Attlee* (London, 1982).

sought – as had been sought before, and would be sought again – agreement between the parties on reform, and on a stricter definition of the power of the Lords. For the moment, however, that formidable statesman, the fifth Marquis of Salisbury, grandson of a great Conservative Prime Minister, and Leader of the Opposition in the House of Lords, enjoined responsible conduct on his followers. Essentially, he asked them to allow into legislation – amended if necessary, but only when the case for amendment seemed to be overwhelming – anything that Labour had put in its manifesto. Speaking to Dr Janet Morgan in 1970[5] Salisbury explained his thinking:

> The Conservative Peers came to the conclusion that where something was in the Labour Party manifesto we would regard it as approved by the country . . . If they produced something that wasn't in the manifesto, we reserved the right to do what we thought best . . . We passed on Second Reading nearly all the nationalization bills – in the one case of the Iron and Steel Bill we went rather further as we didn't think they'd a justified demand. So we put in an amendment not to put it into force till after the election. The Labour Party accepted that.

Such was the conciliatory school of political management in which Carrington earned his spurs; and he liked it. What lay behind Salisbury's thinking on tactics stayed in Peter Carrington's mind for twenty years. So, on becoming Leader of the Opposition in the Lords in October 1964, he told his troops:

> If the Labour Leadership are reasonable, we let them get away with it. They know how far they can push us. Once we start using our veto, we're damaging the object of a Second Chamber. If the House of Lords is to work, we must show forebearance and commonsense.

Two things of importance had happened between 1945 and 1964,

5. Janet P. Morgan, *The House of Lords and the Labour government, 1964–1970* (Oxford, 1975). Dr Morgan's brilliantly concise monograph is required reading for any student of constitutional politics.

apart from the Macmillan government's legislation allowing the disclaiming of peerages. The first was in 1947, when Attlee decided that Salisbury's promise of constructive opposition was insufficient to his purpose. After talks between the parties in 1948 failed to produce a mutually agreeable solution, the Labour government decided to legislate to reduce the period by which the Upper House could delay the implementation of legislation. In 1949, therefore, they introduced a Bill to reduce the delaying power to nine months. This was passed, over Lords' opposition, by means of the provisions of the 1911 Act. The second development was a change in the views of the Labour Party. By 1964 scarcely a member of that party could be found who would support Attlee's belief in the acceptability and desirability of a hereditary peerage. Indeed, large sections of that party required the dissolution of the House of Lords and all its works and pomps. With these developments in view Carrington, who had thought deeply about the matter over the years, and who dearly loved and valued the Second Chamber, had concluded that an advance had to be made from the position adopted by Salisbury. A root-and-branch reform of the Lords had to be undertaken; every possible effort had to be made to bring about that reform by agreement; and in negotiations leading to agreement it would behove the Conservative Party to yield on any point which the Labour plenipotentiaries regarded as essential. It was in this spirit that Carrington began discussions with Richard Crossman, the Leader of the House of Commons in Harold Wilson's first administration, in 1964. The spirit was certainly pessimistic, and was called by his critics defeatist. But it is due to him to note that he believed that, if his line was not followed, the end would be the abolition of the Lords under the 1911 legislation, and that he was prepared to resist by any means available to him. The model he saw and feared was the Labour Bill of 1949: if a Labour government less tractable than that of Attlee chose to use its powers and held – as Harold Wilson did after 1966 – a sufficient majority in the Commons, nothing could save the Lords. Carrington's judgement on all this, as was to be shown, was mistaken, but it was intelligible, and it proceeded from honest feeling. It arose, further, out of his direct personal experience as a Whip organising Conservative forces against the 1949 Bill. The learning of the neophyte of the 1940s issued in the practice of the party leader of the 1960s.

In the 1950 general election the Conservatives came close – closer than had seemed imaginable in 1945 – to reversing their post-war defeat. The senior members of the Labour Cabinet, it should be remembered, had now been continuously in office since 1940. The Tories, for all the anguish they had suffered in 1945, had had a rest from power. Policy and presentation had alike been refurbished. Even so, the Opposition could not take the last fence. The exhausted Attlee government held on, winning a majority of 17 over the Conservatives and an overall majority of only five. Another clash could not be long delayed with Churchill, a revived old warhorse sniffing the breeze of battle, and a host of eager young politicians prepared to stay up night after night at Westminster to batter down the last retaining wall of the Attlee redoubt. Twenty months later, on Thursday, 25 October 1951, the Conservatives came back, 26 seats ahead of Labour, and 17 ahead of the combined opposition parties. They were to hold office, though nothing seemed less certain in the moment of victory, for thirteen years.

In the four years during which he had been a Whip Carrington had won a good, if not exactly a glittering reputation. He could now reasonably expect movement, even promotion, to what politicians generally call a 'real', that is a ministerial job. He was known to, and liked by Churchill who, often, by this stage of his inordinately lengthy career, had only the vaguest awareness of and interest in those minnows inhabiting the lower reaches of government. Carrington made known to Salisbury his desire to 'do something more practical' than being a Whip. He neither expected to be offered what he was offered, nor anticipated the storm that would subsequently arise in the Ministry of Agriculture. Indeed, it appears that he was not even the first choice for the job he accepted. Sir Thomas Dugdale, who was to be Minister, certainly preferred Anthony Hurd – later Lord Hurd, and father of the present Secretary of State for Northern Ireland – who was both a journalist and a farmer. But Hurd declined a ministerial existence and became, instead, chairman of the backbench agricultural committee.

Carrington got the job designed for Hurd, as one of two Parliamentary Under-Secretaries, the other being Richard Nugent. Both junior ministers were without departmental experience and Nugent, indeed, had entered the House of Commons only the previous year. The lack of relevant experience on the part of both men was, subsequently, in 1954, taken sympathetically into account. For the moment it is enough to say that their chief, Dugdale, was a Tory Party warhorse of some experience; but, like his juniors, his experience was not departmental, the highest previous point of his career having been reached when he was, from 1935–7, Parliamentary Private Secretary to Stanley Baldwin. He had much of that celebrated political leader's bluffness, but not much of his judgement. For the moment he gave Nugent (who had previously sat on an important committee of the National Farmers' Union) the responsibility for liaising with the Union and Carrington responsibility for talks with the larger landowners and all those matters involving travel. In practice, this turned out to be a vague arrangement, but Dugdale was pleased to have two such gifted young men working under him (Nugent, at forty-four, was twelve years older than Carrington).

To understand what followed after Carrington had begun the climb towards ministerial power, three things have to be appreciated, and I mention them in order of chronology rather than importance.

First, during the darker stages of the war the government had taken power compulsorily to acquire property which was considered to have potential use in the war effort: as has been observed,[6] by the end of the conflict the United Kingdom was more thoroughly and more collectively organised for war than was Germany. The process of collectivisation was, however, begun before war broke out, and in 1937 the Air Ministry acquired land in Dorset known as Crichel Down, for use as an experimental bomb site. Many other such purchases were made later, but there was a general, if inexplicit understanding that such properties would be available for re-purchase by their former owners, on reasonable terms, once emergency or war was over.[7]

Second, it was an obvious imperative, during the war years, for Britain to produce as much of her own food as possible. Imported food

6. Winston S. Churchill, *The Second World War. iii The Grand Alliance* (London, 1950), p. 113.
7. For what follows I am particularly indebted to Anthony Seldon, *Churchill's Indian Summer: the Conservative government 1951–55* (London, 1981), pp. 219–22. Dr Seldon's pioneering study depends not merely on access to state papers, but on extensive interviews with politicians and civil servants active during his period.

cost money which could be spent on armaments and, as submarine attacks increased in intensity, such imports were in greater and greater danger. There thus began the system of agricultural subvention which persists to the present day, albeit in a massively more elaborate and expensive form. Even when peace arrived the natural collectivist instincts of the Labour government dictated that the wartime system should be developed rather than abandoned. In consequence the Agriculture Act of 1947 (which was less socialist than based on the conduct of the 1940–5 coalition government) ordained both that there should be guaranteed prices and assured markets for farmers, and that relations between government and farmers, founded on the assumption that the state would make up by way of deficiency payments what farmers could not make in the market, should be conducted according to certain rules of negotiation. The Ministry, for its part, was anxious to ensure that the most advanced forms of food production should be encouraged, and offered to put its weight behind experimental schemes. After all, if British farmers could produce better food more cheaply than the farmers of other countries, then they would be in less need of deficiency payments, and the burden on the taxpayer would be correspondingly lighter. On all this Tom Williams, who had been Attlee's Minister for Agriculture throughout the life of the first post-war government, and Thomas Dugdale, were agreed. Personal relations between the two men, and between the members of their respective party committees, were excellent.

Third, while Clement Attlee paid little attention to the machinery of government, Churchill was obsessed, in 1951, with what he saw as the necessity of re-creating in peace the system that had operated so well in war. Although this practice did not last, the fact was that for the first few years after 1951 departments were grouped under overlords who were little in touch with detail and, at the lower levels, responsibilities were rigidly, rather than, as previously, casually divided between junior ministers. It fell out from all this that the papers relevant to what became known as the Crichel Down affair passed over the desk of Carrington, rather than that of Nugent.

What happened was this. In 1950, having no further use for the site, the Air Ministry decided to pass it over to the Ministry of Agriculture, one of whose inspectors had expressed interest in it as a possible site for an experimental farm. All the technical decisions relating to this transfer were taken by civil servants and initialled by ministers, who had forgotten, or had never known of, repeated political assurances that original owners would be given a fair chance to re-purchase compulsorily acquired land. Unfortunately for some of the civil servants and politicians involved in the transfer from one ministry to another, there resided in Dorset a former naval officer, one Lieutenant-Commander George Marten, a man of means, perspicacity and determination. Under the terms of all those vaguely expressed and, by the 1950s, half-forgotten assurances Commander Marten's wife would, being the heiress to a large part of the Crichel Down land, have been offered a chance to buy it at a reasonable – and not necessarily a market – price. Commander Marten went on the attack.

Commander Marten and his ilk fell within Carrington's sphere of ministerial responsibility, insofar as a Parliamentary Under-Secretary can be considered fully responsible for decisions determined at one and the same time by the vagueness of policy on high and by the secret detail of policy determined from below by civil servants. From 1951 onwards Carrington steadily advised his minister that Marten's agitation could safely be ignored, and Dugdale accepted this advice. Marten was not, however, a man readily put off; and his purse was long enough, it appeared, to continue his attack indefinitely.

In October 1953 Dugdale yielded to Marten. Sir Andrew Clarke QC undertook an independent inquiry into the affair. Clarke reported in May 1954. He concluded that there had been high-handed conduct by the Ministry, but that no corruption on the part of civil servants had been involved.[8] On 17 June Dugdale faced his party's backbench agricultural committee, chaired by Anthony Hurd, whom he would have had in his department. The conclusive view from the floor was that, if Dugdale was not prepared to punish the civil servants responsible for a piece of sleight-of-hand in which – it was accepted – he himself had had no major part, he should resign. The House of Commons debated the Clarke report on 20 July, with Churchill present. Dugdale asserted his belief that none of his civil servants had been criminally responsible. He added that, because of the reshuffle following the Conservative election victory of 1951, many of the civil

8. See below, p. 170.

servants who had taken part in the transfer decision of 1950 now worked in other departments. In private he expressed himself grateful that his old Labour opposite number, Tom Williams, had declined to take part in a debate which inevitably assumed the form of a discussion on censure. In public he accepted that the fault was his. He resigned, and passed into private life. His responsible junior, Carrington, likewise tendered his resignation. On being assured, however, that the business was not his fault, he withdrew it. Commander Marten achieved satisfactory compensation: his wife got her land back.

Problems like Crichel Down irritated Churchill as he came towards the end of his final term as Prime Minister. Had he been younger he might have attended more vigorously to the simple theme of justice involved. He wished for no trouble, however, on such domestic matters, being concerned with his last effort to achieve a great peace between East and West through the medium of a summit conference. His views on the morality of the Crichel Down affair were, however, recorded by his doctor. They stand, I believe, as a statement of its essence.

'It would,' Churchill told Moran on 30 December 1953,

> seem proper in the circumstances to return it to its owner, who is asking that his ancestral acres be returned to him, with of course such compensation as may be agreed. But not at all – the government department concerned wants to take it over as Crown lands, though nationalization of land is against Tory policy. It seems to me all wrong. The land was taken for military purposes in a national emergency; it is no longer needed, and cannot be retained for some other purpose.[9]

Dugdale, much later, when he had become Lord Crathorne, described what had happened with an almost endearing simplicity.[10] He said that 'events were very much hurried in that particular year and

9. Lord Moran, *Winston Churchill: the struggle for survival 1940–1965* (London, 1966), p. 517.
10. Anthony Seldon, *ibid*.

again I didn't realise the importance of this particular event down at Crichel and I had more important things to attend to, and I just let it slip by.' Dugdale was not the greatest, nor the most percipient nor the most energetic of ministers but when, in however muddled a way, he came to the conclusion that he had done wrong, he made an according sacrifice.

The hurried events to which Dugdale referred included a considerable expansion of the old Ministry of Agriculture. The new Minister was to be Derek Heathcoat Amory, subsequently Chancellor of the Exchequer, and a man who took pleasure and delight in attending with the greatest care to the minutiae of any job which he was given. Amory was a puritan by nature; and he disliked the whole character and ethos of the department of which he was now given charge: that character, he described in a favourite word of disapprobation, was 'sloppy'. When reviewing the junior ministerial talent available to him with the Whips he made it perfectly clear that he did not want Carrington around.[11]

Fortunately for Carrington, there was a patron at hand.

Harold Macmillan, though formally a Conservative, had been a political rebel throughout the 1930s. At one stage of his life, indeed, his rebelliousness had been so blatant that the Conservative whip had been withdrawn from him.[12] His rebellion had been both against his family tradition, and against the political commitment in which that tradition issued. He had been tempted, against the grain of the Scottish religious world view in which he had been brought up, to become a Roman Catholic.[13] As Conservative member for Stockton he had been appalled by the suffering the depression had imposed on his constituents in the 1930s. He wrote a book on the subject of economic regeneration, *The Middle Way*.[14] At the same time, unlike more calculating rebels, he had opposed with vehemence and eloquence what he saw as the complacency of the Baldwin and Chamberlain governments in the face of the rise of Nazi Germany; and he had thus become an ally of Winston Churchill. Churchill, when he became Prime Minister, elevated this hitherto (by the Tories) despised back-

11. Private information.
12. Nigel Fisher, *op. cit.*, p. 51f.
13. See Evelyn Waugh, *Ronald Knox* (London, 1959).
14. Harold Macmillan, *The Middle Way* (London, 1966).

bencher, and had sent him to North Africa as a minister with Cabinet rank, concerned, above all, with making smooth the paths of relations between the British, the Free French (under Charles de Gaulle) and the Americans.

Macmillan discharged his duties with panache and, even, brilliance. He took only a fitful part in the reconstruction of Conservative policy after 1945. When Churchill returned to government, however, he very shortly found himself committed, as a result of an incautious acceptance by the leadership of the party of a Conservative Party Conference demand to build 300,000 publicly funded houses a year, to discharge a particularly onerous obligation. He sent for Macmillan. Macmillan achieved the magic target. Churchill then, in 1954, moved him to the Ministry of Defence, obviously expecting miracles again. Macmillan asked for Carrington as his Parliamentary Secretary.

Macmillan did not want to be Secretary of State for Defence. His ministry was, to him, something of a backwater. He had gained national prominence as Minister for Housing. He saw himself losing that prominence as an electorate, tired by war and concerned with the reconstruction of the body politic, withdrew their attention from matters of defence. He thought it, moreover, an example of Churchill's failing judgement that the Prime Minister had given as one of his reasons for Macmillan's appointment the new Minister's unquestionably gallant record in combat in the First World War.

Defence was, said Macmillan, 'a queer kind of affair. I have no power, yet I am responsible for everything – especially if it goes wrong', and he complained that, if he asked for a small meeting, 'about forty or fifty people turned up'.[15]

Furthermore, Macmillan was ambitious to demonstrate that, in any department of which he took charge, he could change things, and at speed. Speed and achievement were possible at Housing; they were not possible at Defence, for technical reasons. Macmillan fell back, therefore, on a choice of junior minister which mirrored exactly the Churchillian choice of himself which he upbraided. He selected as his junior in a technical ministry a young man with a good military record and a social conscience. He also told Carrington that he intended to reform thoroughly the Defence Ministry, then a haphazard collection

15. Harold Macmillan, *Tides of Fortune 1945–55* (London, 1969), p. 560.

of departments responsible for the individual services. (He did this when he was Prime Minister, and pulled together all ancillary military ministries into one department.) Macmillan thought that Carrington had been unfairly treated by Amory. Carrington, naturally, responded to that view with favour. The great thing was that Macmillan saw in Carrington somebody like himself.

Macmillan arrived in office in October 1954 just after the completion of a defence review. This further handicapped him in his desire to make an impression. In the nature of the departmental timetable the most that Macmillan could hope for was a three-year slog before he had a chance to present his own defence review. From this dismal prospect he was rescued only six months after his appointment, when Churchill decided at last to retire and make way for Anthony Eden. Six months' acquaintance was, however enough for Carrington to speak in warm terms of that period to Macmillan's biographer, Nigel Fisher.[16] He realised immediately, he said, that he was 'working for an unusual man, both in his quick grasp of problems and in his positive attitude towards them'. Macmillan was to leave his mark, not only on Carrington's thinking, but on his style.

Carrington remained at the Ministry of Defence until 1956 when he was unexpectedly, on Macmillan's suggestion, appointed British High Commissioner in Australia. The period was long enough, however, for him to acquire a wider view of international relations than he had hitherto possessed and long enough, too, for him to acquire certain ideas, and to develop a certain posture in foreign and defence policy, which were to stay with him into maturity.

It was just before Macmillan and Carrington were appointed to Defence that Eden, the Foreign Secretary, had enjoyed a marked diplomatic triumph, one which, as Paul-Henri Spaak believed, saved the Atlantic Alliance, and for which Eden was awarded the Garter. What Eden achieved was full membership of NATO for Western Germany, while at the same time he brought Britain into full membership of the European military alliance. Thus was cemented the grouping of Western nations, under the leadership of the United States, which thereafter would confront the might of the Soviet Union. The post-war alliance was thus given what to all intents and purposes was

16. Nigel Fisher, *op. cit.*, p. 143.

to be its final form. The difficult question that remained to be answered was how the members of that alliance were to be armed, individually as well as collectively.

At a time when there are such sharp differences between a Conservative government and a Labour opposition on the question of British defence strategy, and when that government has seen inroads made into public opinion by the efforts of the Campaign for Nuclear Disarmament, much tends to be made retrospectively – and this was done by Mrs Thatcher's government in the opening weeks of 1983 – of the idea that Tories and Labour were at one over nuclear strategy in the 1950s. For example, just the same dispute over 'first use' of a nuclear weapon arose then as has arisen now, in the debate over the Defence White Paper in February 1955. Labour, it is true, did not criticise the Conservative decision to manufacture the hydrogen bomb, but they sought vehemently an assurance against first use – which the government would not give. Their position was logical: the bomb was considered not merely as a defence against a Russian first nuclear strike, but as a deterrent against a conventional Russian thrust in the central European plain, a thrust which, they believed, they did not have sufficient non-nuclear forces to turn back.

Their decision thus both to build the hydrogen bomb – one not taken at all lightly, taken, indeed, only after the most agonising appraisals in government circles – and not to eschew the right of first nuclear use called into question the whole issue of the value of conventional armament. It is quite clear that Macmillan – and Carrington to the lesser degree that befitted his junior position – felt that the full advent of the nuclear age, summarised by the replacement of the atom with the hydrogen bomb, meant that conventional forces were to become henceforth of far lesser significance. 'It is quite impossible', Macmillan wrote in his diary, 'to arm our forces with two sets of weapons, conventional and unconventional.' And when he became Chancellor of the Exchequer in the Eden government he regarded the sums of money required for non-nuclear defence purposes 'wasted' and 'a great burden on industry as well as on the Exchequer'.

The emphasis thus created, of regarding the Russian threat as the only significant military challenge Britain faced, of believing that it would come in the centre of Europe and that it could only be deterred by nuclear weapons, or only fought with them, has remained with

Carrington. It had a deep influence on his conduct when he was himself Secretary of State for Defence. It influenced his attitude at the Lusaka conference before Rhodesian independence, and caused him to oppose the commitment of British troops on the ground in that country which the Prime Minister favoured. Finally, the perceptions then developed made him impatient with all commitments of a military nature outside the NATO area, something that was of importance in the line he took on the Falkland Islands.

As I have already mentioned, the Carrington family had strong Australian connections, great-granduncle Charles having governed an Australian province, and Peter's own father having been to school there. The only thing about the appointment which excited surprise was the new High Commissioner's youth. However, although there is nothing of significance to record about the three years he spent in Australia, there can be no doubt that he was a great success in what was a tricky, if not exactly an arduous post. It was not merely the eternally recurring sensitivity of Australians to Britons that might cause him trouble, especially considering his title and his age, but also the fact that the world was changing in a way that was bound to affect both the Commonwealth and Anglo-Australian relations. The Australians were starting to look increasingly to the United States for trade and security, and the bonds with the mother country were certain to be weakened. To preserve as much as could be preserved, and above all to preserve the family intimacy that, in spite of many minor tensions, existed between the two countries, was the chief charge laid on the young High Commissioner.

Then, in 1957, the Commonwealth Prime Ministers' conference in London was for the first time attended by a black Prime Minister, Kwame Nkrumah of Ghana. It was evident that, given Britain's declared policy of moving towards independence for most of her colonies, great changes were coming about in the international constellation of states in which men such as Macmillan and Sir Robert Menzies, the redoubtable Prime Minister of Australia, had achieved maturity. None the less, although change not altogether agreeable to such as Menzies was evidently coming, the future seemed bright with hope.

Emboldened by his personal success at the 1957 conference Macmillan decided to launch himself on the first Commonwealth tour by a British Prime Minister, calling on India, Pakistan, Ceylon, Singapore, New Zealand and Australia. This was a trip which, given its outstanding success, was important for Carrington's future. His performance, after all, would be compared by the Prime Minister's critical and sceptical mind to that of such as Malcolm Macdonald, High Commissioner in India, and already a Commonwealth legend, and Sir George Mallaby, the highly experienced and much admired High Commissioner in New Zealand. 'To his genuine surprise,' Carrington told Nigel Fisher of Macmillan, 'he took Australia by storm and got better and better as the tour progressed. He is rather a shy man, but the success of the tour greatly increased his self-confidence.' Macmillan felt similarly about his representative. Carrington, he wrote in his memoirs, *Riding the Storm*,[17] was 'perhaps the best envoy we have ever sent' to Australia. It was hardly surprising, therefore, that on expiry of his term of office in Australia, Macmillan offered him government advancement, and the post of First Lord of the Admiralty.

17. Joseph Godson, *op. cit.* and Harold Macmillan, *Riding the Storm 1956–1959* (London, 1971), p. 181.

4. THE DIFFICULTY

I found Carrington looking rather uncomfortable . . . I told him
exactly what I wanted. He said, 'It's no good talking to me, you
should go personally to Heath and explain it all to him.'

Richard Crossman, *The Diaries of a Cabinet Minister*
(ed. Janet Morgan) vol. iii (London 1977).

In 1959 the Admiralty could not any longer be described as a mighty
office of state. The shadow of Macmillan's reorganisation of the
Service departments and their integration into a Ministry of Defence
where the Secretary of State would enjoy real authority over his
Service subordinates – in contrast to Macmillan himself during his
brief sojourn at Defence – lay over it. But it was a department of
substance. It was a post redolent of history, in general because of the
country's glorious naval past, in particular because it had such definite
associations with Churchill, being the base which he had commanded
at the beginning of both world wars.

Naturally pleased by an appointment that took him straight back to
the centre of things, Carrington was none the less surprised. 'If,' he
said after a year in his new job, 'when I arrived to take up office, you
had spoken to me of a White Ensign, I should have immediately
concluded that you were talking about a rather pale subaltern in the
Brigade of Guards.' Neither three years as a diplomat, nor the assumption of new responsibilities had, clearly, dimmed his wit.

None the less, there was trouble in store for him: as his time at the
Ministry of Agriculture had been clouded by the Crichel Down affair,
his time at the Admiralty, and what he did there in the way of patient
and sensible administration, was dominated by the Vassal affair. And
again, just as he had ignored all the warning signs indicating that
George Marten would be a formidable opponent, so, in the view of
many, he underrated the challenge of an espionage scandal and lost his
habitual finesse in handling it. 'It wasn't,' a contemporary explained
to me, 'that Peter didn't take his job seriously. He did. But he couldn't
really believe all this cloak and dagger stuff. I suppose you might say

that there was a certain carelessness of intellect there.' There was no doubt that that was the view of the press, with whom the First Lord rapidly became deeply and bitterly embroiled.

The Vassall affair was one event in the long line of security scandals which began with the defection of Guy Burgess and Donald Maclean to the Soviet Union and which has continued down to the 1980s, occurring with such depressing regularity that they have made the security services, in the minds of many members of the public, into something of a joke. (Indeed, when Carrington and his senior minister, Peter Thorneycroft, told Macmillan about Vassall he could only say, according to Chapman Pincher in *Inside Story*,[1] 'Oh, that's bad news . . . You should never catch a spy. Discover him and control him, but never catch him. A spy causes far more trouble once he's caught.')

Anyway, the events which were to cause Carrington embarrassment in his time at the Admiralty began in 1961, with the apprehension, trial and conviction of an espionage ring – consisting of a Russian, two Poles and two Englishmen – employed in the Underwater Weapons Establishment at Portland Bill. Sir Charles Romer immediately presided over a committee charged with recommending improvements in security procedures. A month after the trial George Blake, himself an employee of the Security Services, was convicted of espionage and sentenced to 42 years in prison. Lord Radcliffe was then asked to investigate a situation in which, it appeared, British security was being penetrated with almost insolent ease by Soviet agents. Radcliffe's report appeared in April 1962. Like most reports of its kind (one has only to think of Franks on the Falklands) it found nothing seriously wrong. But it did make two recommendations. The first, based on awareness that a number of Civil Service unions had been infiltrated by Communists or fellow-travellers, was to the effect that the political affiliations of those being considered for posts in the public service should be more thoroughly checked. The second was that particular attention, buttressed by periodic vetting, should be paid to anybody whose personal life or predilections might leave him open to blackmail.

From the Portland spy-ring trial onwards there were persistent

1. London, 1978.

rumours both in Fleet Street and Westminster that there was a further spy, in the Admiralty, and that the authorities were being less than zealous in hunting him out, and even less than enthusiastic about implementing the vetting reforms recommended by Lord Radcliffe. In September 1962 the Admiralty civil servant, John Vassall, was arrested on a charge of spying for Russia. It quickly emerged that he had served in the British Embassy in Moscow in 1954 (where, it transpired, he had been blackmailed and recruited) and was a homosexual. It emerged, further, that he had had a brief but close relationship with a Civil Lord of the Admiralty, Tam Galbraith, MP, whose Private Secretary he was, and that he had for some time been living well above his means in London. But from all the accusations of slackness two things stood out: the fact that Vassall had regularly travelled between London and Galbraith's Scottish home with documents that were at least confidential if not top secret, and the extremely dangerous if only implied accusation that Galbraith had enjoyed the homosexual favours of his secretary. In the end the judgement of the Annual Register was most widely accepted. It avowed that 'the most that could be said against Mr Galbraith was that he had suffered a socially pressing and plausible junior colleague a trifle too gladly'. None the less, Galbraith resigned. Carrington did not, nor was it suggested in his own direct circle that he should.

For general as well as particular reasons, the Prime Minister felt it expedient to hold another inquiry, again under Lord Radcliffe: investigation of and gossip about the state of the nation's security were rapidly becoming spectator sports.

Lord Radcliffe presided over fourteen days of public hearings (examining 51 witnesses) and nineteen days of secret session (with 100 witnesses). Press discussion of the whole affair had been fevered, and it rapidly appeared that the truthfulness of newspaper reporting was one of the central issues which the tribunal had to examine. The whole business, indeed, became a sort of trial of moral strength between journalists and ministers. The former were angered by what they took to be flippancy on the part of the politicians towards the affair; but they had also seriously over-reached themselves. Indeed, as the late James Margach, political editor of the *Sunday Times* for many years, later wrote, '. . . the press had plumbed disgraceful depths of character assassination'. Central to the attack on Carrington was the argument put forward by Percy Hoskyns in the *Daily Express* on 8 November 1962, to the effect that the First Lord had known since the trial of the Portland conspirators in 1961 that there was another spy in the Admiralty, but had done nothing about it. For good measure, Hoskyns added a report that Carrington had been carpeted by Harold Macmillan for his carelessness.

Carrington flatly denied both aspects of the report and Mr W. L. Mars-Jones QC, representing Hoskyns's employers, Beaverbrook Newspapers, apologised. Carrington replied, tight-lipped, 'I take note of what you have said.' He added that he had not heard of the possibility of there being another spy in his department until 4 April 1962. Nor, he insisted, had he been dilatory in informing either Thorneycroft or Macmillan as the situation developed. Truthfulness was now central to the inquiry, and, subsequently, two journalists, Brendan Mulholland of the *Daily Mail* and Reginald Foster of the *Daily Sketch* were jailed on the grounds that their refusal to reveal their sources constituted a contempt of court. Thus began a war between Macmillan and the press which resulted in 1963 in the almost universal Fleet Street savaging of that government when war minister John Profumo was discovered to have had an affair with Christine Keeler, and to have lied to the House of Commons about it.

Of 250 newspaper reports he had considered, Lord Radcliffe eventually concluded, not one was justified. The newspapers were severely rapped over the knuckles and ministers were exonerated (Galbraith subsequently returned to office as a junior transport minister). However, the day before the tribunal ended Carrington announced publicly, through his QC, Helenus Milmo, that he would not take a final decision about whether or not he would resign until later. In private, though, he showed himself quite set against resignation. The Radcliffe exoneration settled the matter finally so far as he was concerned: Lord Radcliffe, in the manner of so many similar British inquirers, contrived to find a scapegoat, H. V. Pennells, Civil Assistant to the Director of Naval Intelligence, who was adjudged 'remiss and lacking in judgement' in selecting men to serve behind the Iron Curtain. Pennells was, conveniently, dead.

What the hearings revealed to his friends and colleagues, however, was a quite new Carrington. 'He was so grim', a subordinate of the time said. 'I think he was put out by the fact that he only got the news of Vassall's arrest on 14 September when he was halfway back across the English Channel (from his holidays). He felt that the release of that fact gave the whole thing the appearance of an emergency, when he believed it was just a culmination of routine, a routine investigation. The way it was done made it possible for the press to imply that he was caught on the hop. That made him furious.'

If Carrington did not display fury before Radcliffe, he undoubtedly demonstrated a controlled, glacial anger. It was, in many respects, an impressive performance, one judged so by most impartial observers, though also felt to be one betraying characteristics not heretofore associated with his personality. However, while few of his ministerial colleagues envied him the experience of cross-examination, all relished the adamantine front he presented to the voracious critics awaiting each stage of what, those critics fervently hoped, would be a major unveiling of inattention, if not corruption, in high places.

The fact, however, that the whole business so rapidly assumed the character of a gladiatorial confrontation between the Macmillan government and the press, did conceal one or two matters of more general interest, one of which is of particular interest to the student of Carrington himself. The First Lord had been accused of paying insufficient attention to rumours of the presence of another spy in the Admiralty after the Portland trial. He had averred that the possibility had come to his attention only in April; and from April to September was not an unreasonably long period to be allowed for the necessarily delicate investigation to unmask such a spy.

However, on hearing the news of Vassall's arrest on 14 September Carrington waited until 24 September for a lengthy discussion with Thorneycroft, and until 28 September for one with Macmillan. One of the main reasons for these delays, it seems, is that he was engaged on scrutinising the whole system of Admiralty security, so that he could be completely *au fait* with its structure before reporting in depth to his Minister and the Prime Minister. Now, while it is not at all reasonable to expect a Minister to be in day-to-day finger-tip touch with every section of his department – nor the Prime Minister with the activities of the security services themselves – it has to be remembered that a particular injunction had been laid on the political heads of the Admiralty to review the system after the Portland revelations. What could be said, therefore – and was said in political circles, though not in those of the press, where the mood was now one of suppressed rage and vengefulness — was that Carrington had not yet discharged that duty.

Of course, it has to be remembered, in mitigation of the strength of any criticism of Carrington at this time, that throughout the extraordinary period of the early 1960s, when security scandal succeeded security scandal or apparent security scandal – the Profumo affair was not such, though it was represented as such – the inner attitude of the government was an extraordinarily insouciant one. No one, governing or governed, had doubted that great issues were involved when Donald Maclean and Guy Burgess defected to Russia when Macmillan was Foreign Secretary. But from 1961 on there were the Portland spies, George Blake, Vassall, Philby's revelation that he had tipped off Burgess and Maclean and his immediate departure from Lebanon for Moscow, and then Profumo, sharing a girl with the Russian military attaché. Harold Macmillan's favourite private word for the central characters in all these episodes was 'squalid'. One of his favourite grumbling contentions was that the security services – and, by extension, their political masters – gained no credit and only abuse for the apprehension of traitors and spies. There was, in a phrase, in government circles, an attitude of bewildered incomprehension, directed not merely at the state of affairs, but at the hysterical-seeming press reaction to it. The difference of attitude between politicians and press could, indeed, be put in this way: the politicians never believed the next scandal was going to come; the press were in dispute only about when it would come. Carrington simply went along with what was the prevailing attitude of his colleagues, and particularly of his mentor, Macmillan. He had no conception of how corrosive an agent the question of security would prove to be in the public decay of a government of which he was a member.

That government was already in the closing stages of its life. In 1963, just before the October Party Conference, Macmillan resigned his office upon entering hospital for a prostate operation. The circumstances in which his unhappy affliction enforced this action were calculated to turn the subsequent battle for the leadership into something approaching a Roman circus.

It was, however, a circus in which much of the important action took place in secret, and certainly away from the public gaze. Exactly what happened in the frantic days following Macmillan's resignation has been a matter of dispute between students of the affair from that day to this, but it is fair to say that no serious critic today doubts that Macmillan engaged in intricate manoeuvres to ensure that the succession would pass to the fourteenth Earl of Home, his Foreign Secretary. As it began to be rumoured that Home was a candidate, the Conservative membership of the House of Lords was, naturally, delighted. The Foreign Secretary's chief advocate in the Upper House were Lords St Aldwyn (the Chief Whip), Dilhorne (a former Lord Chancellor) and Poole (a former Chairman of the Party). To such efforts Carrington lent a willing, but junior hand.

Now, Lord Hailsham had already, at the party conference in Blackpool, declared his intention of disclaiming his peerage in order to return to the House of Commons and seek the leadership of the party. He stated, however, that his search for a seat in the Commons (he eventually secured St Marylebone) was in no way dependent on his ambition for the leadership: he wanted to leave the Lords in any event. Then, though it was theoretically and constitutionally possible for Lord Home to become Prime Minister and remain in the Lords, it was felt, in the modern age, to be impracticable. He also disclaimed his title, and was eventually returned for the constituency of Kinross and West Perthshire. The two most prominent and active Tory members having thus abruptly departed, the mantle of the Leader of the House of Lords fell almost automatically on Carrington.

There were, on the face of it, advantages and disadvantages in this elevation, and all arose from the delicate position a peer occupies in any government.[2] It was disagreeable for Carrington to be, again, without a department. On the other hand, the leadership of the Lords brought with it, automatically, a seat in the Cabinet. Douglas-Home, furthermore, designated him Minister without Portfolio – the third such minister in his cabinet, the others being the Chairman of the Conservative Party, Lord Blakenham, and the Minister for Information, William Deedes – and indicated that his duties in that rôle would be essentially concerned with the Foreign Office. Thus was Carrington first brought into intimate touch with the department of state which it was ever afterwards his ambition to lead.

2. Above, p. 3.

Circumstances combined to enable him to make the most of this appointment. Douglas-Home found himself from the beginning in an extremely difficult position. First, he could not possibly form a government without the assent of his chief rival, R. A. Butler. He therefore offered Butler any office he chose to have and Butler selected the Foreign Office, the only major Cabinet post he had not so far held. Second, though he had once been a minister in the Scottish Office, Douglas-Home had virtually no experience of domestic politics: he had to prove himself on unfamiliar ground before a general election. Thus, the minister most experienced in foreign policy could not devote his time to it, and the most intelligent man in the government had to spend time learning the trade of diplomacy. Third, as regards the forthcoming election Douglas-Home decided to make a virtue of necessity. He needed every available moment to get the party back into shape and present himself as a convincing Prime Minister. For that he needed quiet, as well as time. He announced that he would not hold an election before he had to: it was therefore known that the general election would be held in October 1964, the last possible date. This immediately took some of the heat out of a fraught political situation. Carrington began to spend a good deal of his time at the Foreign Office, taking the routine weight off Butler. Other decisions and events were to help him further forward.

It was an important part of the attitude of the Prime Minister to the forthcoming electoral battle that he should continue the conduct, not only of the nation's affairs, but of his own life, as he normally did. When Parliament rose for the summer, therefore, he left London for his estate in Scotland. His initial plan was to spend the whole of the summer there, thus demonstrating a lofty unconcern in the face of the propagandistic vulgarities of Harold Wilson and a confidence – one truly, in his case, unforced – in a Conservative victory come October. Because he was so very new in his position, because his emergence had been so very unexpected, because Wilson had already proved so adept in his coining of phrases and slogans suggesting the inadequacy of the new Prime Minister, it behoved Sir Alec Douglas-Home to act as though he was not merely accustomed to govern, but accustomed to govern as First Lord of the Treasury.

In the event, what appeared at the beginning of the recess to be a cool and settled plan to demonstrate *sangfroid* on the part of a governing party which had been so at odds as to its elements only the previous October dissolved under various pressures. The Foreign Secretary, Butler, was exhausted and retreated first to a Scottish destination – like Home's own – the Isle of Mull, and then to Wales. Enoch Powell once described Butler as the carthorse of government: on an occasion when he was ill, Powell said,[3] the whole machinery of Cabinet committees seemed to come to a halt. Lord Moran, in his much traduced, but remarkably convincing memoir of Winston Churchill, said much the same.[4] But even Butler had to rest occasionally, and it may be that, his second and final bid for the office of Prime Minister having failed, he no longer had either spring or zest.

A second pressure on the government during what was to prove to be, psychologically speaking, an exceptionally long and fractious summer came from the international situation, and particularly that in the Mediterranean. Turk and Greek glared at one another over flimsy barriers in Cyprus, even though both races were nominally allied in a government of the island. Turk and Greek glared at one another, at a longer range, but no less virulently, from Ankara and Athens: the virulence of two NATO governments in actual political and potential military conflict with one another was enough to cause serious concern in every NATO capital from Oslo to Washington, for the Mediterranean theatre was judged to be a crucial one. At the same time, the government of Dom Mintoff in Malta was in the throes of the first phase of what has since come to be seen as a virtually inexorable process: the extirpation of the NATO presence on an island whose population, in recognition of their valour during the Second World War, had received from King George VI the highest possible British civilian award, the George Cross. The conclusion – the ending of military facilities for the NATO navies of the United Kingdom and Italy in the harbour at Valetta – was not seen to be inevitable in 1964. The collective advice of the Foreign Office was that something could be worked out. It was not yet understood, even by the most gifted, that Mintoff had set his face towards a wholly new policy for Malta: he saw its future as lying in alliance with North Africa rather than with Europe.

3. J. Enoch Powell, in *The Listener*, 16 April 1981.
4. Moran, *op. cit.*, p. 449.

The Mediterranean pressures were not, in that summer, such as the Conservative Party wished to consider. What was approaching was a general election; and it would be fought, it was perfectly clear, on the ground of competence and energy, crudely summarised in Harold Wilson's brilliant judgement that the electorate had come to the conclusion that it was 'time for a change'. Far better – so the electoral thinkers of the Party concluded – to consider, not Malta and Cyprus, but Halifax and Huddersfield. The question the electorate would ask was not whether Archbishop Makarios or Raul Denktash in Cyprus, or Dom Mintoff or the Archbishop of Valetta in Malta, were in the right, but whether, after thirteen years of office, the Conservative Party, under a sheltered and untried leader, could beat off, on the ground of domestic policy, a Labour Party reinvigorated by a leader who brought with him the very whiff of modernity and fashion already generated across the Atlantic by the glittering (if later to be proved tawdry) personality of President Kennedy.

But there were still considerations, both of responsibility and of tactics, that required a Conservative government, even in these last weeks before what was expected to be a bitter and gruelling campaign, to give attention to the Mediterranean.

The first was that the major NATO powers – the United States and those on the continent of Europe, excepting Greece – looked to Britain to sort out the problems of Cyprus and Malta. The United Kingdom was the residual colonial power in both islands; and Malta still had a British Governor-General. London was expected – indeed, required – to take the lead in organising an agreement in Cyprus that would prevent a clash between Greece and Turkey, and a settlement with Malta that would ensure the continued availability of the port at Valetta.

The second consideration – one that bore hard upon the minds of Conservative Party managers – was that the one great advantage enjoyed in the domestic political battle was the acceptance by press and public alike that the Prime Minister, for so long Foreign Secretary, was unchallengeable, either intellectually or in diplomatic practice, on foreign affairs. It thus fell out that Home interrupted his holiday no less than four times – while Butler was supine at Mull – to travel to London and lend his weight to Mediterranean argument. In the event, this did no domestic political good at all. Although Home took a train

three times, and flew once, between Scotland and London, this travel-
ling activity neither assisted the Mediterranean negotiations, nor
enhanced his reputation for command.

All this time, however, the centre of British diplomatic activity
remained the Foreign Office, and the central personality became
Carrington. 'It was at that time,' he later told a friend, 'that I knew I
wanted to be Foreign Secretary.' At the beginning of the summer his
position seemed to be compounded of formal dignity and thankless
drudgery. He was Leader of the House of Lords, yes, but Minister only
without Portfolio. He had to discharge conversational responsibilities
with entrenched and excitable politicians from two different islands
without enjoying any real authority. Yet by the end of the summer,
and on the eve of the Tory defeat, there was nobody who did not think
well of him. And when, at the end of the Malta agreement, Mintoff
toasted him in champagne, his refusal to return the toast in kind, as I
have said, preferring port because of a detestation of fizz[5], was taken
by the assembled company to be an assertion of independence which
marked the arrival of a major politician.

In October Home went down to a narrow defeat: he had acquitted
himself – if one considered the chaos and near-despair of the party at
the time of his accession – exceptionally well. He agreed, however,
that the manner of his becoming Prime Minister was not one suitable
to the age, and that the controversy surrounding it dictated a reform of
that system. He thus arranged for the institution of an electoral system
for the choosing of Conservative leaders, but he declined, despite the
urging of his friends, to offer himself as a candidate. He had little taste
for opposition and also, as he told the late George Hutchinson, 'I like
being leader, but not enough to fight for it.' In 1965 he was succeeded
by Edward Heath.

Carrington had, naturally, continued as Leader of the Conservative
Party in the Lords after the election defeat. His assiduity no less than
the personal skill of his diplomacy during the summer of 1964 had
won him golden opinions. Mintoff, Makarios, Denktash and the
governments in Athens and Istanbul all praised him. Butler now decided
to retire from public life and, on the nomination of Harold Wilson,
became Master of Trinity College Cambridge. Douglas-Home became

5. Above, p. 12.

Shadow Foreign Secretary. It was the expectation of the time – though one that time was to disprove – that he would not stay long in active politics. It became conceivable, therefore, that should Edward Heath win a general election Peter Carrington would be near the achievement of what, in the year that saw the fall of the Home government, had become a consuming ambition. He could see himself as Foreign Secretary.

Heath's first try was not, however, a glorious one. In the spring of 1966 Harold Wilson was beset by electoral and parliamentary arithmetic. After the 1964 election he had enjoyed a lead of 13 seats over the Conservatives, but only four over the combined opposition parties. Two of his own members, moreover, had demonstrated their determination to wreck his plans to nationalise the British steel industry. Given the recalcitrance of these two – Desmond Donnelly and Woodrow Wyatt – the government was automatically hamstrung on the implementation of one of its most important manifesto pledges. Assessing the inexperience of the new Conservative Leader, therefore, and calculating that the electorate would give him a real chance to fulfil his promises, Wilson went to the country on 31 March 1966. He emerged from the battle with a majority of exactly 110 over the Conservatives and of 96 over all opposition parties. The situation of 1945 was almost exactly repeated: a House of Commons dominated by the Labour Party confronted a House of Lords just as dominated by the Conservative Party. And the junior Tory Whip of the first period was the Conservative leader of the second.

Heath, quite rightly, had not been judged harshly for his failure in 1966. It was generally agreed, indeed, in party circles, that his final broadcast of the campaign had been an exceptionally impressive one. Paradoxical though it may sound, moreover, there was a certain relief to be got out of the prospect of a prolonged period of opposition. Time would make it less and less necessary to defend the record of the government beaten in 1964. Time would be provided, too, for that thorough re-examination and reconstruction of the party that Heath favoured. Time would make it possible to bring forward new men, and to detach the leadership from the old and the worn-out. Opposition could be principled rather than tactical. A new philosophy, even, might be hammered out. In all this there would, of course, be a rôle of heightened importance for the House of Lords.

Carrington was now almost exactly where Salisbury had been in 1945. If his political ancestry did not have the same lustre he none the less had a firm reputation, and the Crichel Down and Vassall affairs were forgotten. In addition, however, to the repetition of the old problem of being in opposition to a Labour government there was a new problem, volatile in its nature, and guaranteed to excite the most passionate and bitter controversy. On 11 November 1965 the Prime Minister of Rhodesia, Ian Smith, had unilaterally declared the independence of his country from the United Kingdom. Britain, followed immediately by all Eastern and most Western nations, and by the United Nations, had imposed economic sanctions on the government in Salisbury. Wilson had striven to ensure a bipartisan approach to this issue at Westminster, but it was known that a large number – possibly a majority – of Conservative MPs, and a preponderant number of Conservative peers, were opposed to sanctions. Furthermore, the legislation embodying their imposition had to be renewed each year. In addition to his other problems, therefore, Carrington faced an annual test of his doctrine[6] that the Conservative Party in the Lords should proceed with the utmost caution in its dealings with a Labour government. The undisputed personal fact remained, however, that by 1966 Carrington had arrived in the front rank of Conservative politics.

And yet, between 1966 and 1970, it was not in Carrington's area that the Opposition attracted most attention. Heath had two great ambitions, which became steadily more apparent as the gruelling years wore on. The first was to initiate and complete a thoroughgoing reappraisal and reformulation of Conservative policy, atrophied, it was thought, by more than a decade of office. The second was thoroughly to overhaul the management and finances of the party itself, and activity regarded as something of a prelude to the overhaul in office of the machinery of government, a task which Heath regarded almost as paramount, and which provoked him to unwonted passion. The first ambition was the one which attracted most outside attention, right up, indeed, to the 1970 election. It may be questioned, with the benefit of hindsight, how significant all this activity was, particularly given that, from 1972 onwards, the Heath government embarked on a

6. Above, p. 6.

process of steadily renouncing the more radical elements in its 1970 manifesto. Indeed, by the time Heath was replaced as party leader by Margaret Thatcher in 1975 it was one of the most bitterly expressed claims of her adherents that Heath had entirely abandoned the tenets of the 'quiet revolution', the commitment to lead Britain in a radical and libertarian direction which characterised the period 1965 to 1970.

None the less, the commitment in energy and manpower alone to policy reformulation after the 1964 defeat was considerable. At the end of 1964 Heath himself became Chairman of the long-standing Advisory Committee on Policy and in the following years he vastly extended the network of policy groups over which it presided. He was innovative in recruiting outside experts to attend meetings of these groups, not infrequently individuals whose natural political sympathies did not lie with his party. Thus, before the 1966 election there were twenty-three policy groups with a combined membership of 181 MPs and peers and more than a hundred 'experts' from outside. Some groups were then disbanded, but others were created, and between 1966 and 1970 there were twenty-nine of them, with a political membership of 191 and an outside attachment of 190. Although attendance at and output from many of the groups was fitful, considered as a whole they represented a unique effort on the part of a British political party.

The foreign affairs group was one of those disbanded in 1966. The main outlines of Conservative foreign policy were set in stone. No creativity or radical change was conceivable, given Heath's utter determination to establish as *the* objective of foreign policy the entry of Britain into the European Economic Community. To that, everything else – the Atlantic Alliance, the Commonwealth, and the embarrassing imbroglio over Rhodesia – was subordinate, matters merely of local tactics. Ideas on foreign policy that went beyond – or which skirted – the European commitment were not welcomed. The oft-proclaimed willingness of Heath to re-think anything did not apply in this area.

It was possible, even in the second half of the '60s, to be sceptical about the great re-think, for to Edward Heath it was as much an exercise in a managerial streamlining as in philosophy. Carrington was certainly among those politicians – a very markedly Conservative type – who took a humorously jaundiced view of intellectual effort in politics. None the less, the public prominence accorded to the exercise, and the importance attached to it by the Leader, attracted and encouraged to great effort most of those ambitious Tories who sought to impress under the new dispensation, in the post-Macmillan era. Carrington was not among them. As the election of 1970 approached he sat on the Steering Committee charged with advising the Shadow Cabinet on the contents of the manifesto, but that was in any event a necessary part of his duties as Leader of the House of Lords. He took no more than a vestigial interest in the rest of the labyrinthine business of policy formulation.

On the other hand, the managerial reforms going forward attracted him. After the August 1969 Sundridge Park seminar organised for businessmen (and some politicians) whom Heath wished to attract, eventually, into government, Carrington joined, and played an important part in, a committee designed to see that work was followed through on the various projects that emerged from Sundridge. And, in 1967, he took charge of a massive Conservative party fundraising campaign which gave him a good deal of insight into the creaking party machine, and prepared the way for his assumption of the chairmanship in 1972.

His choice of priorities – his decision about where to allocate his own efforts – during these years of opposition underlines important sides of Carrington's character as a politician. Although a politician of instinct rather than ideas, he essentially aspires, given a certain general context of political and social belief – that personally determined for him in the early '50s, and that more generally defined by the fashionable post-war ethics of the '50s and '60s, ethics of an essentially collective nature – to efficient management.

To the Carrington Appeal, designated to rescue Conservative Central Office from the vastly increased expenditure burdens of modern electioneering, and to place its finances on a sound footing, David Butler and Michael Pinto-Duschinsky, in their Nuffield study of the general election of 1970[7] apply the same judgement as they apply to party machinery reforms as a whole: 'it was a negative success'. They add that, '. . . while large resources – in terms of members, agents or

7. See David Butler and Michael Pinto-Duschinsky, *The British General Election of 1970* (London, 1971).

finances – were not built up, steps were taken to prevent them from running down and they were used with greater efficiency ... the Carrington Appeal managed to remedy a potentially dangerous situation but did not raise sufficient funds to permit spending on previous scales.' His experience of the party organisation gained during his work for the appeal, however, gave Carrington a strong distaste for what he considered to be the ramshackle character of Tory organisation, which was greatly to influence him later. (Though it is fair to add that, while there were undoubtedly faults at Central Office, the efficiency and commitment of its staff, and the quality of its methods, made it immeasurably superior to its equivalent at Labour headquarters at Transport House, a fact willingly acknowledged by Labour politicians and officials alike.)[8]

As I have already mentioned, the problem created by the Rhodesian declaration of independence gave Carrington some of his most difficult moments in the House of Lords. Rhodesia, too, was the principal reason why Heath broke with a long tradition of Conservative leadership. Until his election the Leader never attended a party conference. He merely appeared on the last day, as from the clouds, to give an address which was expected to be rousing, and which would send the deferential troops away in good heart for the new political year. But Heath's position was uncertain. He was not merely a new leader, but a new kind of leader. And he faced, from 11 November 1965, the trauma generated by UDI. For there were a substantial number of what might be called the old Conservative right, supported by a new and harsher breed of Tory organised in the Monday Club (which, in those days, had 1,000 national and 3,000 local members) who were determined that the painter should be cut and Mr Ian Smith and his colleagues allowed to get on with matters. For a variety of reasons – faith in the Macmillan record on decolonisation, his own sense of justice, and fear of the reaction of Commonwealth and world opinion – Heath was determined so far as he could to support the Wilson policy of bringing down the rebel government by sanctions, which were, incidentally, supposedly made mandatory by the order of the United Nations. This last international characteristic of the sanctions policy further inflamed right-wing Conservative opinion, for the

8. See Marcia Falkender, *Downing Street in Perspective* (London, 1983), p. 45f.

United Nations was to that section of the party as much anathema as the prating black politicians who continually insisted that Britain should take decisive steps – including, if necessary, military steps – to bring Smith down.

Heath was fortunate in being sustained throughout by the unswerving loyalty of Sir Alec Douglas-Home. Home had immense prestige in the party: some of it derived from his own character and record, but most of it, during the first phase of the Heath leadership, from the impeccable grace with which he had conducted himself since Heath had succeeded him, and his utter lack of rancour at the fact that he had been replaced. (After 1975 Tories in general, and supporters of Mrs Thatcher in particular, were quick to make an unfavourable contrast between Heath's behaviour in that year and Home's between 1965 and 1970.) Again and again Home quelled revolt at the annual party conference. In 1966, against all precedent, Heath felt forced to intervene in the sanctions debate himself: attendance throughout the conference during these years he considered necessary, for general reasons to be sure, but particularly to be on hand in case of a Rhodesian revolt.

Soon after the general election of 1966 the 'usual channels' were opened to facilitate discussion between the parties of the possibilities of reform of the House of Lords. The 'usual channels' is the phrase commonly used in Westminster to describe the occasions on and the methods by which the business managers of government and opposition consult on resolvable differences or common policy. Heath and Carrington alike jumped at the possibility of an agreed policy, for both men felt that the still predominantly hereditary Upper House was an anachronism: even the Macmillan reforms, which had introduced life peers, had failed in their effect. Too many ennoblements still went to ageing and tired ex-ministers. Too many of those recruited from worlds other than the political found it impossible to procure the time to make the expected contribution to political affairs. On the left wing of the Labour Party, moreover, there were those who wanted their Lordships' house abolished altogether, or, at the very least, replaced by an elected Senate. It was common ground between the two front benches that a reform which at least truncated, if it did not altogether abolish, the hereditary element (perhaps by allowing hereditary peers to continue to speak, but not to vote, in the House) was desirable. Some elected element, likewise, was found attractive. But, of course, being practical men, neither Harold Wilson nor Edward Heath were willing readily to abandon the substantial influence which a Prime Minister acquires by his power to nominate peers. On the basis of all these considerations consultation went ahead, Carrington taking the lead on the Conservative side, thus espousing a reformist cause which he has never abandoned, and his support for which, indeed, he has reiterated at every opportunity from that day to this.[9]

In 1969 the Lords' reform proposals were to be abandoned by the Wilson government in the House of Commons because, despite the general support accorded to them by the Conservative opposition front bench, an adamantine alliance between Labour left and Tory right made it impossible to get them through and preserve the government's business timetable (ten days were spent on the first five clauses alone). This revolt was led by Michael Foot and Enoch Powell, who had very different reasons for resistance (Foot was opposed to the increased prime ministerial patronage the proposals would entail, Powell took a sacerdotal view of the House of Lords). In any event, however, formal talks between government and opposition had – much to Carrington's chagrin – ended in the previous year, because of his conduct of opposition policy in the Lords over Rhodesia.

In order to understand what happened the rôle of the House of Lords in the British legislative system must be understood, as must distinctions between different kinds of legislation. Under the 1911 and 1949 Parliamentary Acts the House of Lords have the duty to amend (where they consider this necessary) Bills arriving from the House of Commons, and the power to delay the granting of the Royal Assent to such Bills for a year. However, over this century an increasing volume of legislation is what is called 'delegated'. The delegation procedure works in this way. An Act of Parliament may empower – or require – the relevant minister to bring into force one or more of its provisions on a date or dates after the Bill itself has received the Royal Assent and become an Act. The minister in question does this by means of an Order, or a Regulation. Such orders and regulations are debated by both Houses but, while they may be rejected, they may not, unlike Bills, be amended. Thus, for example, in 1969 the Boundary Commissioners recommended a revision of constituency boundaries which, it

9. Janet Morgan, *op. cit.*

was widely believed, would favour the Conservatives. The Home Secretary, James Callaghan, was under a statutory duty to lay an Order embodying the Commissioners' recommendations before both Houses, something he was naturally reluctant to do. He introduced a Bill to relieve himself of this disadvantageous obligation. The House of Lords threw it out. Callaghan, therefore, in November, laid the required Order before the House of Commons, but used the Labour majority therein to vote it down, thus ensuring that the Labour Party entered the general election of 1970 unhindered by any consideration of fairness in regard to the geography of constituencies. But it was at no stage open to him to amend the recommendations of the Boundary Commissioners.

In the middle of 1968 the Wilson government – and the Conservative opposition – found itself in a much more acute position. Sanctions on Rhodesia had been imposed, not only by the desire of the government, but at the behest of the United Nations. Partly because of the degree of support for the Rhodesian rebels among the British public, partly because Wilson and his colleagues wanted to leave themselves free to sign an agreement with Ian Smith which would not receive the ready approval of the United Nations, the legislation applying sanctions required their annual renewal by Order. When the 1968 Order was laid, however, the pro-Rhodesian Conservative revolt had spread to the Lords.

Carrington decided to appease those of his backbenchers who opposed the renewal of sanctions. He made it clear that he thought it would be highly undesirable for the Lords to veto (they could not amend) an Order which had already received the sanction of the House of Commons, and which represented not only the settled policy of the government but, in principle, the settled policy of the opposition front bench as well (as confirmed, incidentally, by the Conservative party conference the previous October). However, he was prepared to go along with one symbolic vote. But, as he said in his speech on 18 June:

> if in their wisdom the Government decide to re-introduce the Order and it is passed again by the Commons, the factors which I have mentioned in my speech would certainly weigh very heavily with me in any further advice I was bold enough to give your Lordships.

In other words, next time around – and there was certain to be a next time – he would urge the House to support sanctions. This he duly did, with success, a month later. In the meantime, under severe pressure from significant elements of the Labour Party to whom the issue of sanctions was a paramount one, the Prime Minister broke off talks on reform of the Lords.

It is a moot point whether a continued intimacy between the two front benches would or would not have given a fairer wind to the Labour government's proposals for Lords' reform the following year. However, to put intimacy at risk, for the sake of allowing a futile gesture which could easily have been aborted, was an act of less than consummate political management.

There is no doubt, however, that in his day-to-day handling of his followers in the Lords, Carrington won golden opinions. More important, his intimacy with Heath grew, and if he often expressed unease and doubt about what his position would be in a future Conservative government – particularly when he was consigned to such thankless and mundane jobs as the chairmanship of the Questions of Policy Committee, as described later[10] – it seemed that something substantial would certainly come his way.

Between the autumn of 1969 and the summer of 1970 the opinion polls, for long favourable to the Conservatives, began to oscillate, and rumours grew stronger to the effect that the Prime Minister planned a summer general election. Carrington, close though he had grown to Heath, began to express a certain amount of nervousness about his own prospects. He had had, he felt, a good period since 1964, both personally and politically. He had acquired several directorships, for the most part of banks, and had become chairman of the Australia-New Zealand Bank. He had firmly rejected overtures made to him to accept the post of Governor-General of Australia, preferring to commit himself to the hope of major office in a Conservative government. His difficulty was that, as plans were made and refined for a general election campaign, he could see no major rôle being outlined for himself, for all that he had been a popular and successful party fundraiser.

In addition, he was perturbed by the fact that there were a number

10. Below, p. 88ff.

of critics of his rôle as Leader in the Lords. 'After all,' he said in one debate, 'it is not your Lordships' fault that you are unreformed.' He was correct, of course, to blame the failure of the ambitious schemes he had concocted with Richard Crossman partly on the resolute opposition that those schemes had excited in the House of Commons, and partly on Harold Wilson's decision to break off inter-party talks on the subject after he had postponed the implementation of the Rhodesian sanctions Order.

But he had invested a great deal of political and emotional capital in the plan to reform the Lords. The basic scheme had been hatched in the fertile brain of Richard Crossman, but Carrington had found it very nearly satisfactory. He had, with perfect reason, looked forward to being regarded with respect as a man who had been of major help in achieving an objective that had defeated the best efforts of politicians since the nineteenth century. And he was bitter about what he regarded as a betrayal of him by Labour: it seems he did not believe Crossman's assurance to the effect that Wilson had made the decision to end the talks without consulting him.[11] He was aware, however, that those who favoured the reform scheme blamed him for allowing the Rhodesian vote to go ahead, and that those who opposed reform were also those who were in any event sharply critical of what he considered to be his gentlemanly and statesmanlike conduct of affairs in the Upper House.[12] He presented an assured front to the world; he felt he was capable of great things; he wanted only to be given the chance. But when Wilson finally announced that he was going to the country Carrington could still not be certain that he would, in the event of victory, be given what he considered to be his due. His fears were unfounded. On the morrow of his spectacular and, by press and pollsters alike, completely unexpected victory, Heath invited him to become Secretary of State for Defence. Carrington thus returned, fourteen years after he had left it, to an old department, not, this time, as a junior, but as its chief.

11. R. H. S. Crossman, *op. cit.*, volume iii, p. 110.
12. Dr Morgan is particularly critical of Carrington's tactics in the Rhodesia vote.

5. THE DEFENCE OF THE REALM

You'll have to keep your fingers crossed for me,
For see, my mighty predecessors stand,
Great admirals and statesmen, fearfully
Marking my wandering course, my 'prentice hand.

You'll have to keep your fingers crossed for me
When jokes fall flat, and explanations fail,
And all my enemies announce, with glee:
'The man's a flop, and all his cracks are stale'.

But keep your fingers crossed for Britain too,
And all the people that her island breeds;
Her foes so many, and her friends so few
God grant we all may live to serve her needs.

From, Quintin Hogg 'Song for a new First Lord', in
The Devil's Own Song and other verses (London, 1968).

When he became Secretary of State for Defence Carrington did rather more than reach the highest point of his career so far. He had confirmed acceptance of him as a Conservative – and thus a national – political figure of the first rank. There is a nice distinction between figures of influence in politics, and figures of power. The Leader of the Conservative Party in the House of Lords is, of necessity, an individual of influence in that party's counsels. So, for that matter, is the Chairman of the Conservative Party. But unless either of these offices of dignity are attached to the governance of a department of state, they are held only on the sufferance of the national Leader of the Party (the actual, or potential Prime Minister). They have no weight in themselves. If a senior minister chooses, or threatens, to resign, a Prime Minister may fear, or a government may feel threatened. But if an individual, however respected, however able, is, in his office, purely a creature of the Prime Minister or Leader of the day, then he cannot be imagined to possess any real share of power. Being Secretary of State for Defence, and thus administering one of the major spending

1. The 37-year-old High Commissioner to Australia.
(*Press Association*)

2. The grim First Lord of the
Admiralty arrives at the Radcliffe
Commission in February 1963.
(*Press Association*)

3. The man determined to reform the
House of Lords, and the Leader of the
Opposition in that House, 1969.
(*Press Association*)

4. The Shadow Cabinet on 20 May 1970. Lord Carrington is on Edward Heath's immediate left; Mrs Margaret Thatcher on his far right and in the centre of the picture. (*Press Association*)

5. Dr. Helmut Schmidt holds forth to Lord Carrington in Bonn on 15 June 1970. (*Keystone*)

6. The Secretary of State for Defence seems to be enjoying a ship-to-ship passage on 24 July 1973, during a Nato maritime demonstration off Scotland. (*Keystone*)

7. From left to right: Lord Carrington, Dr Josef Luns, Mr Dom Mintoff. On 21 January 1972, in Rome, Carrington and Luns had done a great deal to keep Malta within the NATO Alliance. (*Keystone*)

8. Carrington speaks, Heath listens, at the Conservative Party Conference, Blackpool, October 1973. (*Conservative Central Office*)

9. Sir Alec Douglas–Home returns to the House of Lords after twelve years, sponsored by Lord Balerno and Lord Carrington. 'Alec', said Carrington, 'had come to his senses.' (*Press Association*)

10. Carrington applauded for a speech on Rhodesia at the Conservative Party Conference in October 1979 both by the Chairman of the Party, Lord Thorneycroft, and its Leader. (*Conservative Central Office*)

11. Rhodesia becomes Zimbabwe. From right to left at the table: Robert Mugabe, Joshua Nkomo, Sir Ian Gilmour, Lord Carrington, Bishop Abel Muzorewa, Dr Ndabininge Sithole. (*Central Press*)

12. Lord Carrington attentive, Mrs Indira Ghandi pensive. The picture was taken in January 1980 in New Delhi when Carrington was trying to persuade the Prime Minister of India that the Russian invasion of Afghanistan was a matter of serious concern. (*Keystone*)

13. June 2, 1980. The Prime Minister having achieved a settlement on the contribution of the United Kingdom to the budget of the EEC, three Ministers who had thought she could not win leave No 10, Downing Street. They are Lord Carrington, James Prior and Sir Ian Gilmour. (*Central Press*)

14. Turning Rhodesia into Zimbabwe was difficult. The end of one country and the creation of another was celebrated on 19 April 1980 by, from right to left, the Foreign Secretary, Lord Carrington, the Governor, Lord Soames, and the new Prime Minister, Mr Robert Mugabe. (*Press Association*)

15. The Secretary-General of NATO holds forth on his appointment. (*Keystone*)

departments of government,[1] Carrington moved from being a politician without (of necessity) an electoral base, one who could alter policy or tactics only by the exercise of personal charm, sound argument or persuasion of one kind or another, to being a man of substance in his own right.

His reaction to what had happened in the hours following Edward Heath's general election victory was summarised on an apt occasion, and in an apt fashion, by himself. Both on the day before and on the morning of election day he had been genuinely gloomy. The signs for Heath were black. Carrington thought it a wretched prospect for the country (his was an entirely unselfish point of view) that Harold Wilson should continue in office. He also had to think, reasonably, of himself. A second electoral defeat would shatter anew the still frail unity the Conservative Party had achieved since 1966. Heath was only the second party Leader of the century who had come into his office when the Tories were not in power,[2] the first being Andrew Bonar Law. He would not have a residue, either of affection or prestige, to fall back upon. 'It will be hell in the Lords if we lose,' Carrington told a friend in St Stephen's Club on Wednesday. He meant, of course, not just that all the old problems – that of Rhodesian sanctions and those of opposition to Socialist legislation – would come up again, but that the Labour government (if such there was) would renew its assault on his own House, this time in the certainty that it could make its will prevail through the operation of existing legislation. Did, he, the friend asked, now regret that he had declined even to consider being Governor-General of Australia? Carrington did not reply.

On Saturday, of course, these mopings had been put aside. Heath had kissed hands on his appointment as Prime Minister and First Lord of the Treasury. The sixth Baron Carrington was Secretary of State for Defence. The experts of the opinion poll industry, and of Fleet Street, had been confounded. Moreover, the government's majority in the

---

1. Next to social security, defence expenditure is the highest for government even today. See Peter Riddell, *The Thatcher Government* (Oxford, 1983), pp. 112–19.
2. Austen Chamberlain's experience was unique. He became Leader in 1921. The Party was in office, but serving in a coalition government under David Lloyd George. A year later Chamberlain was overthrown. He is thus the only Conservative Leader this century never to serve as Prime Minister.

Commons – of thirty overall, and 42 over Labour – promised a comfortable legislative life ahead. No wonder, then, that when he saw a television report of the Queen's progress at Ascot racecourse on Saturday Carrington should exclaim, 'All's well with the world. The Tories are in power and the Queen's at Ascot.'

The contrast between his often morose mood during the campaign and his euphoria once it was over shows only that he has natural feelings of depression and exhilaration – ranges of feeling as great as those of most leading members of the Opposition as battle raged between Labour and Tory parties during that (from the point of view of judgement of the weather) halcyon summer of 1970. In the middle week of the campaign, for example, Heath was, for a day, reduced to incapable despair: though he has since denied this, and insisted that he was confident throughout, I know that reports of his depression were true; and that he showed himself to be a braver and bigger man by the way in which he came out of his low period to fight and win so gallantly in the last week.[3]

In Carrington's case those temperamental swings can, of course, be put down in part to the fact that, as a peer, he was neither in the centre of the battle for the nation's mind, nor crucially influential with those who were. He had seen, as recounted in the last chapter, how tactical planning for the election did not provide for him any major rôle for himself. He was asked merely to become, for the duration of the campaign, Chairman of the Questions of Policy Committee. He was dissatisfied, and felt spurned. As it happens, however, I saw a good deal of him in that rôle and it seems appropriate to set down here an appraisal of Carrington in action at the beginning of his time as an unquestionably major Conservative politician.

Carrington has never been a man to decline a task, and certainly not out of pique. The Questions of Policy Committee, however, which exists only during a general election campaign, is an outfit far less grand than its title would suggest. It consists of a gathering of relatively senior party figures *not* – and in Carrington's case the negative must be emphasised – directly involved in the major issues of the

---

3. Heath's position was made manifestly more difficult by the huge popularity enjoyed by Enoch Powell, then still a Conservative, but openly critical of the Heath leadership. See John Wood (ed.), *Powell and the 1970 election* (London, 1970).

general election campaign of the moment. It is usually chaired by a peer. It meets each morning at the headquarters of the Conservative Research Department: in 1970 these were in the tranquil reaches of Old Queen Street, a short walk from the Houses of Parliament, and a brisk one from Conservative Central Office in Smith Square, where the Leader holds his (or her) press conferences during a general election campaign. There it considers requests for information and guidance on matters of policy thrown up all over the country, farms the inquiries out to relevant Research Department experts (usually, though not always, young graduates with an enormous appetite for work, cutting their teeth on politics), considers their draft replies, which are required to be returned the same day and contain accurate reference to relevant documentation, such as front-bench speeches from both sides of the political divide, and distributes the replies to *every constituency* by the evening post.

Work on, or for, the Committee is, usually, paralysingly boring. The grand questions of policy, on the economy, or defence, or education, or whatever, are all settled as far as possible in the manifesto, and candidates can be expected to be familiar with them, and with the answers to them. However, every candidate is plagued by a host of minor issues, and beset by hordes of special-interest lobbyists, from the Lord's Day Observance Society to the various temperance leagues, from anti-blood-sports and anti-vivisectionist campaigners to pro-and anti-abortionists. The distribution of such pressure, all over the country, is uneven, but there is invariably a measure of co-ordination between those asking the questions. A trick question on family law asked of a candidate in Glasgow may be fired the following day at another candidate in Bath. To procure, therefore, both virtually instant response and blanket coverage the policy briefing note supplied to Glasgow automatically goes out to every constituency headquarters in the country. Overall, the operations of the Questions of Policy Committee, for all the trivial-seeming products of its work and the work of those who serve it, provide an awesome example of the exceptional and remorseless efficiency of the Tory electoral machine.[4] But the work of being its chairman is hardly exciting or fulfilling for a man with his hopes set upon a great office of state. We saw a certain

4. Marcia Falkender, *op. cit.*

small glimmer of interest in Carrington's eye if country matters were discussed but, for the rest, he simply did his duty. I thought his stewardship in many ways remarkable and, indeed, admirable, particularly considering he clearly felt he was underemployed.

One of the matters most frequently raised with candidates was that of birth control. Attendant on it was the issue of the so-called population explosion.[5] One Saturday morning during the campaign I – a young desk officer – dictated a brief on the subject, and included in it an attack that I thought slashing on Mr Douglas Houghton (now Lord Houghton of Sowerby) the Chairman of the Parliamentary Labour Party. Houghton was exceptionally prominent in the family planning movement. He had uttered dire warnings about the British people failing to pay attention to the dangers of a population exploding out of control: he used, indeed, such words.[6]

My brief to Carrington and his Committee, in response to a question about the attitude and policy of the Conservative Party towards State-subsidised birth control, roundly asserted that Houghton's policies, taken to their logical conclusion, would result in the government of the day taking steps, whether by way of reward or punishment, to compel acquiescence with a favoured birth-control policy. The brief was seen and passed by the Committee and duly circulated around the country.

Then the roof fell in. By what means nobody knew a copy of the brief fell into Houghton's hands. He was both affronted and furious. He telephoned Carrington, announced that he was consulting lawyers, and demanded a public and prominent retraction of what he asserted was a libel on his character and beliefs. Carrington sent for me. He asked, initially politely enough, what hard evidence I had for what he now saw to be (though he had not seen it when he passed the brief) a remarkable slur on a respected elder statesman of the govern-

5. It is difficult nowadays to recall the intensity which the debate on population *in Britain* reached at this time. To some degree it was a part of the burgeoning debate on the environment. Only the previous year the Conservative Party had appointed its first Research Department desk officer concerned with environmental problems.
6. The significance of Houghton's intervention lay not only in his position as Chairman of the Parliamentary Labour Party – one very similar to that of the Chairman of the Conservative 1922 Committee – but in the high regard in which he was generally held in public life.

ment party. I had only recently taken over responsibility for family policy from a departing colleague and my acquaintance with the files was less than minute. I was certain, however, that at least one speech by Houghton bore the interpretation of his views that I had put forward in my brief. The trouble was that the relevant file could not be found.

Carrington was enraged. 'Everything that could go wrong with this campaign is going wrong,' he snarled, 'and now I have to face the consequences of your incompetence.' His fury was, on the face of things, more than justified. I was naturally distressed at the embarrassment I had caused him. He saw my distress and immediately changed tack, setting himself to allaying it. Gently, but searchingly, he probed me on the background to the brief and he offered to stall Houghton for a time to see if I could come up with the missing file or, indeed, anything hard in the way of evidence. In due course my hyper-efficient secretary[7] discovered some newspaper clippings reporting an angry exchange between Houghton and Harold Wilson in which the Prime Minister made accusations not dissimilar to my own. I took these to Carrington.

His delight was manifest and his subsequent performance masterly. He invited me to wait while he telephoned Houghton. With the cuttings on the table before him he proceeded, so it must have seemed to Houghton, to make every conceivable attempt to wriggle off the hook of embarrassment which his adviser had fashioned for him. Houghton did not relent, however, and when the game had run its course Carrington gently interjected the Wilson cuttings – in sum, various reports of a letter he had written – into the conversation. His triumph – and, vicariously, my own – was complete, and Houghton retired, presumably in some discomfiture. Carrington hooted with boyish laughter, clapped me on the back, offered me a drink and talked to me of politics for some time. He was engaging, witty, and cynical by turns, but I was fully aware that he was thoroughly and considerately setting himself to making up to me for his short temper over what was – at least in the documentary inadequacy of my original brief – a blunder on my part. His capacity and willingness to take that kind of care over personal relations, however fleeting they may be, is

7. Miss Vanessa Taylor, now Mrs Merfyn Bourne.

one of the things that has won him the enthusiastic and undying loyalty of almost everybody who has worked with him for any length of time. There are two men I know who are regarded as having hypercritical minds, and tongues to go with them. One worked for Carrington in his capacity as Chairman of the Conservative Party, the other when he was Foreign Secretary: neither will hear a word of criticism of him.[8]

Nearly all the salient elements of Carrington's personality are evident in my account of him as Chairman of the Questions of Policy Committee, and they are evident in their common proportions to one another. There is the slight carelessness in passing the original brief, unaccompanied as it was by hard evidence, and the willingness to trust a subordinate untested. There is the short explosion of temper, rapidly succeeded by the emergence of an irrepressible kindness. And there is the mischievous humour of his handling of Houghton.

Again and again throughout his career all these elements come, one after another, to the fore. Indeed, his offhand humour is one of the things – along with the absence in his make-up of that hard and occasionally frantic ambition to be found in most senior politicians – that has often led colleagues and opponents alike to underrate him. When he chaired his first meeting of his service advisers at the Ministry of Defence he opened the proceedings by saying, 'Well, gentlemen, what are we defending?' In the pause which his remark was designed to produce he added: 'And what are we defending it with?' 'He's just a layabout', said one general afterwards; but that general had undergone the most searching scrutiny by Carrington, and he had not come well out of it. He preferred, therefore, to attempt to guy the Secretary of State with a kind of flippant naivety, partly because he did not realise that the opening questions were profound as well as simple, and partly because he had not relished the closely hatched series of questions that had followed them.

Carrington saw, immediately, one serious problem about the work of his old department, and that of the NATO Alliance. The problem concerned the procurement of weaponry, and of the ammunition and spare parts which were required to make existing weaponry efficient.

8. The same favourable view is taken by Brenda Sewill, certainly the best Director the Conservative Research Department has ever had, and its chief in 1970.

Then – alas, as now – there was a constant competition between the sixteen member-nations of NATO to provide machinery for the whole alliance. In theory if, say, Italy – the country which produced the Pucara aeroplane for training pilots – produced the best 'plane, then every NATO airman ought to train on Pucaras. If it became necessary – if, that is, there was a military crisis in Europe – to supply Canadian and United States forces flown in from across the Atlantic with spares and ammunition, then those spares and that ammunition should be available, and immediately, on the ground in Europe. As things stood in 1970, however, they were not.

Carrington therefore asked his Prime Minister if, when nominating for Heath's approval his own Minister of State, he could choose a man who would spend his whole time seeking to achieve a rationalisation of weapons and supply procurement. Heath gave Carrington a free hand, and Ian Gilmour became Minister of State at the Ministry of Defence with particular responsibility for what became known as the Defence Procurement Executive.[9] The creation of the DPE which, even today, is of an uncertain effectiveness, is the sole fact to be recorded about the three years Carrington spent at the Ministry of Defence.

'When he left,' said one general who had taken a personal liking to Carrington, 'we missed him just about as much as a bucket of water misses a hand withdrawn from it.' To some extent, of course, Carrington in 1970 was the victim of the system that had disillusioned Harold Macmillan in 1951. 'The Ministry of Defence,' says one expert, 'is about the only department in Whitehall that takes forward planning seriously.[10] It has to, because of how weapons systems are produced. First of all you have to identify strategic and tactical requirements. Then you have to say what *kind* of weapons system is needed to meet them. Then you have to invite competitive designs. Then you have to wait for the blessed things to be manufactured. It is extremely difficult, if not altogether impossible to interrupt the chain of events between the first and the last stages. If you do interrupt it

9. Gilmour made sterling efforts, but at the time of writing the Western allies are still locked in intense rivalry over efforts to standardise equipment. The difficulty lies not so much in different perceptions of need by military men, but in the inevitable rivalries between different national arms industries.
10. Colonel George Richey. See Patrick Cosgrave and George Richey, *NATO's strategy: a case of outdated priorities?* (London, 1985).

then you get confusion, and sometimes chaos. If the decision to interrupt is taken, also, you will have to be prepared to live with the fact that for some time there will be a gap in the meeting of your defence requirements. Very few politicians will accept that fact.'

Of all defence ministers since 1945 students of military history say that only two – Duncan Sandys (January 1957–October 1959) and Denis Healey (October 1964–June 1970) – made a major impact upon the department, and upon the armed services. There is much dispute about the wisdom of what they did. There is, in particular, criticism of Sandys's obsessive concentration on providing the means of nuclear retaliation against attack, at the expense of conventional forces, and of Healey's rundown, in deference to budgetary requirements, of reinforcement and supply services. But 'both men came to the department with a very clear idea of what they wanted to do. To have an effect a defence minister must work out his policy – his strategy, if you like – before he takes office. Then he must have the gall to force it through. It's too late to start thinking of a strategy even by the time you put your bottom on the ministerial chair'.[11]

All that Carrington had sought to do during the first period of Harold Wilson's primeministership derived from his perception of the dangers to the House of Lords arrived at twenty years previously. All that he sought to do at the Ministry of Defence between 1970 and 1974 was to implement the drive to greater efficiency in government which was the hallmark of Edward Heath's ambition, and in which he had become so interested during the years of opposition.[12] 'I doubt,' says Colonel George Richey who, in 1973 was serving on the Plans and Operations Division of Northern Army Group, 'whether anybody below the rank of Major General even knew who he was.'

There was, however, a reason other than the inherent intractability of his department and the nature of his own temperament which, between 1970 and 1974, drew Carrington away from an exclusive, or radical preoccupation with defence. That was his growing intimacy with Edward Heath, and his increasing influence on the general policy of the government.

Their alliance surprised many who knew both men. Heath, even in

11. Nigel Fisher, *op. cit.*
12. Above, p. 10.

the time of his power, was angular, brusque and less than eloquent. Carrington was relaxed, gracious, and the most entertaining of companions. The opposite poles attracted one another. Every Prime Minister has what is in vulgar parlance called an 'inner cabinet', a particular group of ministers who share his – or her – perception of the problems of the day and with whom he – or she – feels socially comfortable. That James Prior, who had been Heath's Parliamentary Private Secretary, the lowest and most thankless form of official life at Westminster, was translated instantly to the Cabinet as Minister for Agriculture in June 1970 caused few eyebrows to be raised. After all, Heath trusted him implicitly. That Anthony Kershaw, Heath's other PPS, was given merely a junior job at the Department of the Environment ('the ministry of public lavatories and twerps', as he engagingly described it) likewise caused no surprise. Kershaw[13] was outgoing, even flamboyant.

He was not thought to be typical of, nor a desirable representative of the new and (in a vogue word of the time) meritocratic Toryism. That Peter Walker, first as Minister of Housing and Local Government, then as Secretary of State for the Environment, finally as Secretary of State for Trade and Industry, should have the ear of the Prime Minister was certainly no surprise. Like Heath, Walker had made himself into a formidable politician despite having no initial advantages, financial or social, and his best-known business partner, Jim Slater, had advised Heath on the best way to nurture initially very modest monetary resources.[14] Carrington was an unexpected peacock in this otherwise sombrely hued aviary.

Moreover, the rhetoric with which Heath took power was not, on the face of it, readily appealing to Carrington. It was tough, and by some judged harsh. The Shadow Cabinet seminar on policy at the Selsdon Park Hotel at the end of January 1970 had led Harold Wilson to coin the hostile phrase 'Selsdon Man', in which the name of the hotel was taken to be a synonym for 'Neanderthal'. The discussions during the seminar, designed principally to ensure that all those often apparently disparate parts of policy which had been adopted since

13. Now Sir Anthony Kershaw, and Chairman of the House of Commons Foreign Affairs Committee.
14. Jim Slater, *Return to Go* (London, 1974).

1965 were blended into a coherent whole, were in fact quiet and responsible in tone. But, as a strikingly effective act of political propaganda, two of Heath's advisers, (the late) Michael Wolff and Geoffrey Tucker (then Director of Publicity at Conservative Central Office) provided a statement for the press which laid heavy emphasis on law and order, action to be taken on squatters, changes in trade union law, and a clampdown on what was already called 'social security scrounging'.[15] 'It all makes me shudder', said Carrington, contemplating the newspaper headlines on Monday, 2 February 1970.

Again, on the face of it, Heath had grounds to be dissatisfied with Carrington by the middle of 1970. Not everybody was as pleased as Carrington himself with the results of the so-called Carrington Appeal, to raise £2,000,000 to replenish the party's treasure chest. Resentment had grown in the breasts of the executives of several constituency parties whom Carrington had publicly upbraided for their failure to fulfil their designated quotas, and while that resentment was directed as much at the party chairman, Anthony Barber, as at Carrington himself, it was potentially damaging. Heath had conflicting reactions to the whole question of party organisation as the 1970 election drew closer. Instinctively he approved of the tough line Barber and Carrington took with financially recalcitrant constituencies. On the other hand, as any leader in his position would, he feared that public rebuke would lead to a loss of doorstep enthusiasm when the election came.

Then there was the question of the delays and confusions attending the question of House of Lords reform. True, it was Harold Wilson who had unilaterally broken off talks on the subject.[16] True, again, it was the Wilson government's timetable that had been interrupted and, indeed, disrupted by freelance backbench opposition in the Commons. But there was a strong feeling abroad that Carrington had showed a great deal less than his reputed political finesse in his dealings with Richard Crossman and in his assumption that Labour would deliver the agreed reform package in the House of Commons however the Lords acted on such matters as Rhodesian sanctions. But untidiness annoyed Heath and, moreover, he had taken particular

15. David Butler and Michael Pinto-Duschinsky, *op. cit.*, pp. 129f.
16. Above, p. 81ff.

pride in his efforts to present himself as a responsible rather than a fractious Leader of the Opposition: the (to him) futile wranglings over the place of the Upper House in the constitution represented yet another distraction from the business of tackling the causes of the British illness.

None the less, there were important points of contact on policy between the two men. If he did not share what often seemed to be the extravagance of Heath's enthusiasm for British membership of the EEC (which took place in 1972) he understood the fundamental argument perhaps better than any other member of the Cabinet, and he was whole-hearted in his support of the Prime Minister's determination to secure entry. Then, as time passed, changes of stance on Heath's part in areas of domestic policy brought him and Carrington closer together, so much so that by the end of 1973 the Secretary of State for Defence was probably the closest of the Prime Minister's advisers.

Carrington, as I have explained, disliked the rhetoric and a good deal of the substance of the Conservative Manifesto of 1970. For one set of domestic proposals, however, he had positive feelings of support almost as strong as those of its creators. This was the draft legislation on the reform of trade union law. This elaborate edifice of provisions for bringing the British trade union movement within the law, and for ending the anomalous mass of extra-legal privileges which had become attached to trade unions over the years, was, essentially, the brainchild of Stephen Abbott at the Conservative Research Department. It was enthusiastically recommended first to the electorate and then to Parliament by Heath himself, by his Secretary of State for Employment, Robert Carr (now Lord Carr of Hadley) and by the Attorney General, Sir Geoffrey Howe, who steered the requisite bill through the House of Commons. Like many voters, and like practically all members of the Conservative Party, Heath and his immediately concerned ministers were affronted by trade union privilege. But they also saw reform as a necessary prerequisite of their drive for greater national efficiency: the pragmatic considerations were as important in their minds as those of principle. To Peter Carrington, however, the matter of principle was uppermost. To him it was, indeed, a question of proper social order.

From the beginning of the government's life to its end Carrington supported the principles of the reform of trade union law, and deplored the failure of the Act to be effective. In another area of domestic policy, moreover, the Heath government changed front when, in 1972, it abandoned the programme of monetary austerity on which it had been elected, adopted a compulsory incomes policy (in defiance of one of the most specific of its pledges in the 1970 manifesto), and embarked on schemes for massively increased public expenditure. The 'U turn' of 1972 (as Harold Wilson described it) was, to Peter Carrington, admirable evidence of an ability on the part of Edward Heath to face unpalatable facts and draw the necessary conclusions from them. The strengthening of the alliance between the two men was signalled by the contemporaneous appointment of Carrington (with Jim Prior for his deputy) as Chairman of the Conservative Party.

This was an appointment of the greatest importance in Carrington's political career, and it was to be the instrument of his influence on government policy at a crucial moment in modern British political history. Though he had described it as 'eighteen months of eating for the party' he had enjoyed his stint – starting in October 1967 – as a special fundraiser. In its course he had learned a good deal about the grass-roots organisation of Conservatism; while he did not always like what he saw he had gained a shrewd appreciation of strengths and weaknesses; and he was provided, for the first time, with a political base other than that of the House of Lords. The *Daily Express*, on 8 April 1972, the day after the announcement of the reshuffle that brought Carrington to Smith Square, pronounced him 'A Winner for the Tories', describing his appointment as 'a brilliant stroke'. In rather more circumspect style David Watt in the *Financial Times* on the same day made the direct connection between previous fundraising and present control of the party organisation. In time it was to be seen as a job which won him as many enemies as friends. He attempted, for example, to ensure that the appointment and payment of constituency agents should be arranged from Conservative Central Office. This offended against the cherished independence of constituency parties. It upset agents who had been particularly well-treated by their local associations, even if it pleased the badly paid: the former group did not like the idea that pay and conditions should be controlled by an unknown London bureaucracy. Finally, it was seen by some members of Parliament who dissented from the government line on one matter or another as the prelude to an enforcement of conformity with the wishes of the leadership on all Tory candidates and sitting members. Carrington strenuously denied that he had any such intention: but the experience of – to name only two MPs – Neil Marten in Banbury and Richard Body in Holland-with-Boston, both of whom were determined opponents of British entry into the European Economic Community, lent convincing colour to the accusation. Marten and Body subsequently believed that they owed their survival only to an announced determination to resign their seats and fight as independent Conservatives at by-elections in the event of their being disowned – at the instigation of Central Office – by their constituency executives. However, and in spite of these more or less subterranean mutterings, the public face Carrington presented as party chairman was an attractive one; and it made a pleasing contrast to the often dour visage of a Prime Minister who once honestly confessed to the trade union leader Jack Jones, 'I am a bad communicator'.

Discontent with Carrington's attempt to complete the streamlining of Central Office and the party in the country begun by Edward du Cann in 1963 and continued by Anthony Barber between 1967 and 1970 was of less importance for the future than the fact that the Chairman was now and of necessity the recipient of all the views, doubts, hopes and fears of active Conservatives around the country. In the winter of 1973 his ready attention to his party sources led him into a course of action that proved inadvisable. The fault in judgement lay in the fact that Carrington, hitherto from his position in the Lords having a cloistered view of public opinion, imagined that having acquired access to the thoughts of Tory party members he had also been made privy to the mind of the nation.

This is not the place for a history of the Heath government, a government which looked at the beginning as though it represented a brave attempt to break with the deadening consensus of post-war British politics[17] and looked, at the end, a tattered remnant of itself in 1970. It is necessary, however, to pick out at least some of the elements in the framework of the political situation as it was between October

17. See Jock Bruce-Gardyne, *Mrs Thatcher's first administration: the prophets confounded* (London, 1985).

1973 and February 1974 in order to understand what Carrington did and why he did it.

'It is our contention', wrote Dr David Butler and Dr Denis Kavvanagh,[18] 'that in the last analysis the election of February 1974 was called by the miners and that the circumstances of its calling decisively affected the nature of the campaign.' With this contention I agree, but there were other elements in the political equation in the winter of 1973–4, some of them of a highly personal nature, which influenced the course of events.

The objective facts are simply and quickly set down. Having in 1972 decided, after all, that an incomes policy, reinforced by statute, was a necessary instrument of government, the Heath government adopted such a policy in 1972: by 1973 it was in its third phase. Given the earlier passage of laws restricting union privilege the government therefore found itself fighting the same enemy on two fronts. It was this experience, and the memory of it, that later persuaded Mrs Thatcher that it would be wise, in a period when wage increases were being deliberately kept down by simply refusing to provide the money for them, to go exceptionally slowly on the reform of the law relating to trade unions. In 1973, therefore, Heath was doubly embattled.

Circumstances, some of them of his own making, were, further, against him. The National Union of Mineworkers were preparing for a bitter and, if necessary, protracted struggle with the government. Joe Gormley, the NUM President, was quoted (though the accuracy of the quotation was disputed) as saying, in words that were to be echoed by his successor, Arthur Scargill more than a decade later, and were echoed at the time by Michael McGahey, his Scottish deputy, that the object of industrial action in the coalfields was not merely to win a pay award outside the terms of the official incomes policy, but to effect a change of government. As the quarrel between government and miners intensified the third Arab-Israeli war broke out in the Middle East. For some days its outcome was uncertain. In order to influence the views of Western governments the Organisation of Petroleum Exporting Countries announced an immediate cut in oil production. In a decision ever to be regarded as both brave and honourable the Dutch government refused to alter their pro-Israeli line of policy, even

18. David Butler and Denis Kavanagh, *op. cit.*, p. 29.

though they were immediately denied all supplies of Middle Eastern oil and the so-called 'spot market' in Amsterdam had to close. As now, Amsterdam was then the centre of the international oil trade, and the benefit of the spot market's existence to Holland was considerable. At the same time, in a decision ever to be regarded as shameful, the Heath government bowed to Arab pressure and refused to allow American aeroplanes, flying supplies to Israel, to refuel in this country. They went, indeed, further: spare parts for Israeli military equipment, ordered in Britain and already paid for, were prevented from leaving the shores of the United Kingdom, although the movement of supplies to Arab countries was in no way hindered. This contemptible behaviour was followed by an outcome it richly deserved. The Dutch bought oil from Nigeria and the United States. A British government seeking to curry favour, and engaged in a conflict of the greatest seriousness with the workers in its most important energy-generating industry, received no favours at the hands of the Arab nations, and gained not a single barrel of oil more or less than it would have done had it kept its pledged word to Israel.

However inept his response to the Arab-Israeli war was, however, Edward Heath could not fail to appreciate the fact that the Arab oil embargo immediately and significantly strengthened the bargaining position of the NUM. Since North Sea oil had not come on stream, he was in a position markedly weaker than that of Margaret Thatcher in 1984: coal had not been stockpiled, and Heath did not have the option, available to her, of instantly switching power stations from coal to oil. It was at this moment, in October, that Peter Carrington began to think favourably of an early general election.

Heath did not start, and could not have wished for, the war in the Middle East. But some of his troubles were unquestionably of his own making. First, there was the fight on two fronts, which I have already mentioned. Second, there was the fact that, though his government had already been beaten by the NUM over a pay dispute in 1972, he had not engaged in the stockpiling of coal with a view to waiting out any succeeding conflict. Third, he started, late in 1973, to understand the bitter consequences of an incomes policy with a prolonged life. The idea of incomes policy – summarised in the slogan 'fair shares for all' – as practised by both Labour and Conservative governments since the war, invariably commands instant public emotional support. The longer the policy is kept in being, however, the more elaborate is the machinery required to enforce it. As that machinery grows in complexity the government of the day finds itself drawn into closer and closer scrutiny of the details of even the most insignificant pay claim. The government, in a word, becomes more and more collectivist, and finds itself taking more and more decisions in areas where it has neither knowledge nor expertise.

Two moments from the campaign due to end on 28 February 1974 illustrate the kind of difficulties in which an over-interventionist government is apt to find itself. On 21 February the Pay Board, a body set up by the government itself, announced, in the person of its deputy chairman, Derek Robinson, that, having re-examined the statistics involved it was clear that miners were less well off than had hitherto been presumed, and that the NUM's case was, in consequence, very much stronger than the government had admitted. Then, on 26 February, Mr Campbell Adamson, the Director-General of the Confederation of British Industry, told a managerial conference that neither he nor his organisation thought much of the government's Industrial Relations Act. Heath was responsible for neither of these statements, but the unpalatable facts remained that he had created the Pay Board and that the public saw the CBI as being the pro-Conservative spokesmen for industry. If the miners could, after all, have had more money, without any very special strain on the exchequer, and if the Industrial Relations Act, probably the central proposal of the 1970 election manifesto was, after all, of little practical use, then what was the election all about?

The fourth circumstance over which Heath could have exercised important influence, if not control, was the concatenation of political challenges. The miners, victorious in 1972, determined yet again to increase their income substantially, threw themselves into the breach as the shock troops of the labour movement. But there were other discontented workers, especially the two rail unions. So far as pay policy was involved the spectacle was rather as described by Sir Frederick Corfield, one of the hard-line supporters of the 1970 manifesto, dismissed in 1972 from his post in the Department of Trade and Industry. 'Ted', said Corfield, 'is sitting on a bubbling pot that's about to explode.'

I record here my belief that the Heath government was brought down by its own internal contradictions. I said so at the time.[19] The contrast between the policy promised in 1970 and the policy on delivery in 1972 and 1973 was so great as to amount almost to a breakdown in the thinking of government. I record here, also, my belief that Enoch Powell, who declined to stand as Conservative candidate in his old seat of Wolverhampton South-West in February 1974 had an important, and perhaps even a vital influence on the outcome of the election through his plea to the country, in Birmingham on 23 February, to vote Labour (on the grounds that a Labour government *might* withdraw from the EEC), just as he had had an important influence in 1970 in persuading the country to vote Conservative.[20] Certainly Powell, in his letter to his constituency chairman resigning his place in Wolverhampton, cruelly exposed the inadequacies in the government's logic.

The election will in any case be essentially fraudulent, Powell wrote,

> for the object of those who have called it is to secure the electorate's approval for a position which the Government itself knows to be untenable, in order to abandon that position subsequently. It is unworthy of British politics and dangerous to Parliament itself to try to steal success by telling the public one thing during an election and doing the opposite afterwards ... I personally cannot ask electors to vote for policies which are directly opposite to those for which we all stood in 1970 and which I have myself consistently condemned. I shall not therefore be seeking re-election for Wolverhampton South-West.

For ten days after this missive Powell was silent. During that time, however, Heath, having started the campaign with a trenchant call to the populace to decide, in the words of one of his slogans, 'Who governs Britain?' announced to an uncomprehending public that, once

19. Principally in the columns of the *Spectator*. See also my *Margaret Thatcher: a Tory and her Party* (London, 1978), and *Thatcher: the first term* (London, 1985).
20. It is a curious thing that Mr Powell, who can justifiably argue that he had a material influence on the outcome of two general elections – those of 1970 and February 1974 – tells me that he has never, privately, correctly guessed a contentious general election result.

returned with a larger majority, he would meet, and make a deal with Joe Gormley. His campaign thus fell between two stools. Those who thought that though he enjoyed a substantial majority in both Houses of Parliament he was right to appeal to the country – using a general election as a referendum – for an emphatic endorsement of the decision to take a stand against the threats of the NUM, symbolised by the power cuts and the three-day week announced on 13 December 1973, were bitterly disappointed by the seemingly flaccid undertaking to negotiate an agreement with Gormley during the campaign. Those, on the other hand, who thought that conciliation and reconciliation were always the best way forward in political affairs were put out by the strident tone of challenge which marked the opening days of the campaign, and not placated by the professions of goodwill towards trade unions in general, and the miners in particular, which marked the middle phase of that campaign. Being uncertain which sector of the electorate he was appealing to Heath tried to satisfy all. He ended up by satisfying none.

Not everybody at the centre of politics, of course, saw matters as clearly as did Enoch Powell. What is now clear, however, is that the crucial influence of Heath's decision to appeal to the voters more than a year before he had to, in circumstances (the Queen being in Australia and having to cut short an official tour in order to appoint as Prime Minister whoever won the battle of the polls) suggestive of panic, was the judgement of Peter Carrington. He was thus important at a critical and historical moment not merely because the years had drawn him closer to Heath, but because, for various reasons, the personal balance of power within the cabinet had changed between 1972 and 1974.

When he won the leadership of the party in 1965 Heath appointed Reginald Maudling as Deputy Leader.[21] In 1970 he made Maudling Home Secretary. During the first conflict between Heath and the NUM in 1972 Maudling advised conciliation and, indeed, surrender.[22] His advice was accepted. In the same year, however, he felt obliged to resign from the government because of police scrutiny of his

---

21. It is important to understand that, unlike its equivalent in the Labour Party, the Conservative Deputy Leadership is not an elective post. The Deputy Leader therefore has no power base outside the will of the Leader.
22. Reginald Maudling, *Memoirs* (London, 1978).

financial affairs: as Home Secretary he was the ultimate chief of the Metropolitan Police Department; he could not, he felt, continue to discharge his duties in that capacity. The soothing voice of Maudling was lost to the councils of Heath.

Heath had been Harold Macmillan's Chief Whip. On his assumption of the leadership in 1965 he had appointed as his Chief Whip William Whitelaw, perhaps the most effective of the many who held that office during the course of the present century. As Chief Whip Whitelaw won a notable reputation for his ability to persuade. By 1972 the situation in Northern Ireland, where trouble had begun with civil rights demonstrations in 1969, had become fraught. Heath moved Whitelaw from the Leadership of the House of Commons — which job he had received after the 1970 victory as a reward for his years as a Whip — to the new post of Secretary of State for Northern Ireland. By a process which an Ulster politician by no means friendly to Whitelaw described as 'alchemy' Whitelaw had, by 1973, procured the agreement of Protestant and Catholic leaders, particularly Brian Faulkner the Unionist and Gerry Fitt the Catholic, to join together in an executive charged with governing the province. No British minister before or since has come anything like as close to procuring peace in the province. For the moment it scarcely seemed to matter that Faulkner's Unionist and Fitt's Republican colleagues disowned the executive. Given time, it was widely believed, it would work. So – this was the idea that suggested itself to Heath – if Whitelaw could bring the Irish together could he not persuade the trade unionists to come to a settlement with the government? In October 1973 Heath decided to move Whitelaw to the Department of Employment.

Unfortunately, the appointment was held up. There was trouble in Northern Ireland, and Whitelaw took the view that he should remain in his post until its most obtrusive manifestations had died down. On 2 December, however, it was at last announced that he would take over the Department of Employment, and be replaced in Belfast by Francis Pym. Whitelaw wanted time to appraise the problems of his new job. 'I need to feel my way into it', he said. But time was a commodity in short supply. Inflation was threatening to become rampant. The balance of payments, approaching a deficit of a billion pounds for the last quarter of 1973, was disastrous. And Joe Gormley and the National Union of Mineworkers were, so to speak, encamped outside the Prime Minister's door. When Whitelaw advised, above all things, against an early general election it was said by those most devoted to Heath, first that his expressed desire for time to play himself in at the Department of Employment was a statement of political egotism, and second that he wished to avoid an early election because the likely results in Ulster would demonstrate that the voters in the province had no confidence in his executive: this proved to be the case on 28 February when the executive was destroyed. The first motive, I am convinced, had no part in Whitelaw's thinking. The second had. The suppositions about both, taken together, led some to the conclusion that he was self-interested.

The ministers close to Heath at this time included Whitelaw and Carrington, but also Anthony Barber, James Prior and Peter Walker. Prior, it has to be remembered, was Carrington's deputy at the Conservative Central Office. 'The miners', Prior told a Press Gallery lunch on 6 February 1974, 'have had their ballot, perhaps we ought to have ours.' This sufficiently indicated where Prior stood on the question of an early election. Two other ministers – Sir Alec Douglas-Home and Robert Carr, the new (from December) Leader of the House of Commons – expressed no opinion, because they did, as they said, not trust their own opinions. Either, or both, could have had an influence upon the decision eventually taken. Neither used their weight.

The battle for the Prime Minister's ear was, therefore, between Whitelaw and Carrington. Whitelaw, for the reasons already adumbrated, was against an early appeal to the country. 'What would we be doing it for?' he asked his friends. But his advice was to a large extent discounted, as I have just explained. That left Carrington, as the most senior of the Prime Minister's advisers, who had a clear view of what ought to be done. As Secretary of State for Defence he had become alarmed by a prospective and drastic shortage of oil: ships might not sail, aircraft fly, or tanks move. As Chairman of the Party he was hearing, again and again, the plangent cry of constituency executives through the country that their desire to see their government put the issue to the touch with the National Union of Mineworkers should be made manifest in a general election.

For the first half of 1973 he had humorously dismissed the idea, put to him by some of his advisers, and by many whom he met on his national tours, that there should be a general election. Yet, as the year advanced, advice offered and instinct felt coincided. Carrington was, quite genuinely, alarmed. He was also exhilarated.

It is the business of those who work for a political party for a salary always to look coldly at the tactical advantage that the party may enjoy, or be able to arrange, at the expense of its opponents. Between October 1973 and January 1974 it was, therefore, not surprising that no less than five reports arrived on Carrington's desk suggesting to him that he ought to advise the Prime Minister that it would be wise to ask the country for a verdict on Heath's stewardship at an early date. The Labour party was in (its usual state of) disarray. Harold Wilson could not decide whether to endorse Joe Gormley's stand, or to repudiate it. The political climate looked reasonably fair for a government more than halfway through its term. In by-elections Berwick-on-Tweed had been lost. But the Conservatives had won in Edinburgh North while Govan, an ancient Labour stronghold, had been lost by that party to the Scottish Nationalists. The weather was not unfair. It gave joy to the party professionals when on 8 January 1974 Heath announced a new disposition of government. A new department – of Energy – was to be created. Its chief would be Lord Carrington. He would get to work immediately. The three-day week was well in force. Power cuts were known throughout the land. Carrington judged that it was possible to move to a four-day week but he was handicapped in his activity because his new department scarcely existed. It was being scrabbled together from various parts of Whitehall. There was a bit from Trade and bit from Industry. The Scottish Office, too, wanted their say, for the oil supplies that might circumvent the coal miners would be drawn from the sea off the shore of Scotland. 'Let's do something', said Carrington, not to the civil servants hastily gathered together in his new department, but to the men and women at Conservative Central Office. They arranged a visit to an oil rig. 'What we want is some peace', Carrington told journalists, just after that visit. What we want, he said in effect to the Prime Minister, is an election which will confirm our mandate.

As I have said, Whitelaw took an opposite view. He was by no means sure that the government could win a general election. His nose, he said, told him that their majority was in danger. Anthony Barber, the Chancellor of the Exchequer – but, for the question at issue, more important as a former chairman of the party – spoke to some of those agents who had assisted him in the 1970 campaign and told Heath that the outcome of an electoral challenge would be uncertain.

Neither Heath nor Carrington could believe it. Public opinion polls showed the government in a position that was unusually favourable, given the economic crisis and the fact that they were well into their term of office. All the noises Carrington heard from the constituencies suggested desire for electoral combat. All the noises heard by Whitelaw in his own constituency of Penrith and the Borders suggested defeat. Whitelaw, however, was uncertain. He was sensible of the accusations that, either to build upon his own political reputation, or to ensure the continuation of the Ulster executive, he wanted to put off a fight on industrial relations and economic policy. Later, and of the decision to hold an election, he was to say, 'Do you remember Churchill? He said about the appeasement people that they looked for peace and got war. Ted's looking for war and hopes he'll get peace. But he'll get war.'

By this time – January 1974 – Carrington was almost beside himself in his desire for a general election. He had seen what a proper Department of Energy could look like. He saw that between his fingers lay the economic future of the country. He had no interest in the intellectual and moral confusion which Enoch Powell had spelt out. Again and again he said to Heath that it was necessary to seek approval for many things: the third phase of the incomes policy of 1972; the essentially just nature of the Industrial Relations Act; the continuance of government by the Conservative Party. Heath yielded to Carrington's imprecations, rather than attending to Whitelaw's doubts. On Thursday, 10 February 1974 Heath telephoned Harold Wilson and Jeremy Thorpe to inform them that he had asked the Queen, by telegraph, in Australia, to agree to the dissolution of Parliament. The Queen accepted the advice of her Prime Minister.

'Well, I don't think we'll win,' Whitelaw told a friend over lunch on that day. Without having reasoned it all out the Secretary of State for Employment had taken the same view as Powell. The government enjoyed a comfortable majority in the House of Commons (as well as in the Lords). There was no pressing *need* for a general election. There was nothing particularly new to say, no shining standard to which to repair. There was nothing, further, to stop the continuance of government. All these things Whitelaw saw.

At the centre of the disagreement – personal relations remained happy – on public affairs there sat the Prime Minister. Dr Butler and Dr Kavanagh[23] were puzzled by his apparent inanition; they described it as follows:

> He disliked the idea of an election fought as a confrontation. His temperamental desire to make decisions slowly and not to show his hand was very evident. People close to him were genuinely confused about his attitude, and worried that he seemed so much off form. During the final discussions [on the miners' and other pay claims] the TUC leaders were baffled by Mr Heath's silences: they found him brooding and uncertain. A trade union leader described him as 'a worried man looking for certainty'.

Hurd has described, in even more graphic detail, the languor of the Prime Minister at that time.[24] No one on his own staff could be certain when he would issue an order. None of his political colleagues could know the direction in which his mind was moving. For the first time since the general election of 1970 civil servants received back from the Prime Minister despatch boxes containing documents which were innocent of annotation. 'Is it that he's hibernating?' one official asked his minister as winter drew in.

We now know that Heath was ill, suffering from a deficiency in the activity of his thyroid glands, a correct diagnosis of which was not made until much later. During the first week of the February campaign it was noticed that Harold Wilson, like his rival, was also distinctly off-colour: he was making the best of a battle with a nasty bout of influenza. The most challenging, and in many respects the most interesting of post-war British general election campaigns was therefore entered upon with the two potential Prime Ministers well below their best form.

Carrington, on the other hand, was at his most energetic and dominating. He had one great advantage, both over his own leader and over the principal spokesman of the Labour Party. He had a

23. David Butler and Denis Kavanagh, *op. cit.*, pp. 37f.
24. Douglas Hurd, *op. cit.*, p. 47.

natural, and quite unforced conviction that the national interest required a general election. He was certain that the Conservative Party would emerge victorious from the struggle. He was, in many ways, the mirror-image of Enoch Powell. Where Powell was utterly convinced that the calling of a general election was wrong, Carrington was just as utterly convinced that it was necessary. Whitelaw, for all his doubts about the likely outcome of an appeal to the people, lacked the blazing conviction of his fellow-counsellor. Thus it came about that a supine Prime Minister and a reluctant Leader of the Opposition (for Wilson did not believe that he could win a general election in 1974) were drawn into combat at the polls by a man who never had faced, and never needed to face, an election in his life.

By the evening of 28 February it was clear that while the Labour Party would not enjoy a majority in the House of Commons the Conservative Party held less than the confidence of the people. While in 1970 the Tories had won 330 seats as opposed to Labour's 287 (with 13 seats shared between the Liberals and other minority parties) in February 1974, 297 Conservatives were returned, as against 301 Labour members. There were 14 Liberals in the new House, and 23 others. However the democratic pack of cards was cut, and even if there was no Labour majority, Heath and his party had lost. Harold Wilson retired to his house at Great Missenden, and remained silent over the weekend. Heath summoned Jeremy Thorpe, the Liberal Leader, from Devon to London, and sought to put together a coalition government. Thorpe was willing, but his parliamentary colleagues were not. On Monday, therefore, Heath resigned. Later that day, at Conservative Central Office, Carrington, asked what had gone wrong replied, curtly, 'We lost', in much the same tones as twelve years later and à propos of the Argentinian invasion of the Falkland Islands he told Robert Kee that '. . . it turned out that we were wrong . . .'

Harold Wilson formed a minority government. In October, however, in pale imitation of his own action in 1966, he sought a genuine majority. The general election of that month saw the return of 319 Labour members, but only 277 Conservatives. There were 39 members from other parties, but the brutal fact remained that, the matter having been put to the touch twice in the same year, the Labour Party emerged from the second election with a Commons majority over all others of three. The writing was on the wall for the leadership of Edward Heath.

It is interesting, and even remarkable, to note that Carrington's influence had increased rather than diminished between February and October. Neither he nor Heath were under any illusion that the Conservative Party was likely to emerge, in a replay of the February election, with a majority in its own right. What, at best, could be hoped for was a hung Parliament in which the party, allied with others, could provide the better part of a government. The confident tones of the February search for a clear mandate dissolved, in October, into an appeal, in the words of a Tory party poster, for 'A VOTE FOR NATIONAL UNITY'. Asked by Robin Day on the BBC programme *Panorama* on 8 October whether this meant that Heath would be willing to stand aside for another Prime Minister Carrington replied:

> I think that is a question that you must ask Mr Heath. But one thing I do know . . . is that he would never put his own personal position before the interests of the country.

This was an intelligible approach, but it was not the stuff to give the troops. Just as, in February, Heath had begun a campaign with a clear and definite call for an increased majority and allowed that appeal to be dissipated, so, in October, it became apparent that the Conservative leadership had no real confidence in itself. The fact that the leaders of all the competing parties – Labour, Liberal, Scottish Nationalists, Ulster Unionists and, even, Plaid Cymru – dismissed out of hand any proposal for a coalition with Heath demonstrated the futility of the Tory appeal.

Some of Heath's supporters took the view that an expression of willingness to serve under another Prime Minister would demonstrate his statesmanlike character to the nation. Others felt, quite simply, that a leader had to lead, and that to suggest even for a moment that he was less than confident of the outcome of the election would discourage his supporters in the country. Carrington was the most prominent member of the first camp, Peter Walker of the second. William Whitelaw havered, for he was acutely aware of speculation to the effect that if the Conservative Party was the largest in the new Parliament, though without an overall majority, the allegiance for a time at least of the smaller parties could be acquired if he were to replace Heath. When it came to the crunch nobody in the higher echelons of the Conservative Party had any hope of victory; and nobody except Heath himself and his closest adherents were sure that they wished him to continue as leader. Carrington, however, had the courage, on election day, to travel down to Sidcup – Heath's constituency – and suggest to him that if he were defeated he should surrender the leadership of the party. Heath declined to consider this suggestion and remained in place, with Carrington's loyal support, until he was overthrown by Margaret Thatcher the following year.

The story of the fight for the leadership of the Conservative Party between October 1974 and February 1975 has been told and retold. Suffice it to say that while in private Carrington confessed his opinion that Heath would not, and could not convincingly, lead the party into a further general election, in public he stated, again and again, his support for the Leader chosen in 1965. When Margaret Thatcher became Leader he concluded that the days of his preferment were over. He continued as the Tory Leader in the House of Lords. In the House of Commons Reginald Maudling, John Davis and Francis Pym all succeeded one another as Shadow Foreign Secretary, but Carrington felt that whatever hope he had entertained of occupying the office that he most desired had to be put aside. He did not, himself, seem to grasp the fact that his suspicion and even fear of the military and political pretensions of the Soviet Union were such as to place him high in Mrs Thatcher's esteem. In 1979 he was delighted – 'flabbergasted is the word', he told George Hutchinson – to be invited to assume the office of Foreign Secretary.

6. THE OFFICE

'The Ministry of Agriculture looks after farmers. The Foreign Office looks after foreigners.'

Norman Tebbit, 1980

When Carrington entered the Foreign Office in May 1979 – to the chagrin of Francis Pym who, as Shadow Foreign Secretary, had fully expected the appointment – he assumed a unique political position. More than any other office of state – with the uncertain exception of the Prime Minister's own – the Foreign Office has acquired over the centuries an aura, a glamour, a seductive quality which the divesting of empire has done little to diminish. Moreover, he was fulfilling an ambition he had openly declared himself to have almost since he entered politics after the war. 'It is the best job in the world', he said more than often, until one day when he was forced to declare, 'It *was* the best job in the world.'

'In my experience', Roy Hattersley, the writer and Labour politician who was once himself a junior Foreign Office minister, told Peter Taylor of the *Sunday Telegraph*, 'it is more often right than wrong on the issues that affect us, but the Foreign Office finds it difficult to believe that it *can* be wrong.' Hattersley believes, moreover, that, 'With the exception of the Quai d'Orsay, the Foreign Office is on the very borders of contempt for the people with whom it does business. It is contemptuous of other domestic departments, contemptuous of the management of British industry, and contemptuous of British governments of all persuasions.' Peter Jay, the former financial and television journalist, who was briefly Britain's Ambassador in Washington during the life of the Callaghan government and the tenure of the Foreign Secretaryship of Dr David Owen, is less complimentary, and just as harsh:

In my experience it is by and large not true that a home civil servant will carry his doubts about Ministerial policy to the point of saying: 'It is my solemn duty as a citizen to ensure

that the Minister's policy is not fulfilled and that mine *is*
fulfilled, whether or not the Minister can be induced to agree
with it'.

Jay believes that in the Foreign Office, 'there is a sincere and idealistic
belief that they are the custodians of the fundamental truths of British
foreign policy, and that the politicians who come and go are among
the nuisances they have to deal with in their lives'. Of the origins of the
Falklands crisis he observes, 'Despite the fact that successive Governments had only agreed to negotiations on the clear proviso that
eventually they would be subject to the wishes of the islanders
themselves, they systematically acted on the basis that that condition
would not apply.' Jay believes that the ultimate cause of the war was
'understatement'.

Carrington inherited a staff of somewhat more than 4,500 people
(including overseas representatives) and a budget somewhat in excess
of £200,000,000 a year. His was not, then, an empire in comparison to
other departments, particularly, say, the department nearest to his in
function, that of Defence, with its budget running into billions and
getting on for 200,000 men under arms subject to its command. What
the Foreign Office undoubtedly is (and its admirers agree this as much
as its detractors) is an empire of the spirit, possessed of an inherited,
acquired and cultivated sense of its separateness and its unique
quality.

All such senses of exclusiveness are potentially dangerous. Even a
healthy rivalry, a burning competitiveness in the seeking of distinction, can teeter over into self-absorption on the one hand and a bitter
determination to obtain primacy on the other. We have seen this in
recent years, for example, in the battles between the services over their
budget appropriations. It is not new. The Royal Navy set itself to
strangle the infant Royal Air Force at birth after the First World War,
and a subsequently powerful Royal Air Force returned the compliment later in respect of the Fleet Air Arm.

None the less, there is a sense in which it is quite reasonable to assert
that the effective conduct of foreign policy requires an entirely differ-

---

1. This was part of a major survey of the workings of the Foreign Office carried out
by the *Sunday Telegraph* just after the Argentinian landings.

ent set of talents from the conduct of domestic policy; and the same applies in reverse. The sad spectacle of Herbert Morrison, domestically a powerful politician, struggling with British foreign policy after the retirement of Ernest Bevin, or that of Anthony Eden buried in the morass of domestic reconstruction in the 1950s when he became Prime Minister, offers telling examples of the dichotomy.

Apart from the matter of personalities, however, the separation of kind between foreign and domestic policy is real. To be sure, post-war governments have found, at an accelerating rate, modern society considered in its domestic character, and the modern political system, singularly resistant to reform. The fate of successive would-be reforming governments – those of Wilson, of Heath, and of Wilson again – is enough to demonstrate that; and the jury is still out on the Thatcher government. There are a host of reasons for this, among them certainly being the excessive desire of modern governments to take to themselves more and more rôles, to aspire to a greater and greater degree of control, to set themselves up as ever more ambitious social engineers. It still remains that a trade union, say, an industry, a company or a particular social pressure group is a subject different in kind, and presenting problems different in kind, from a foreign government, still more from a constellation of foreign governments, whether friendly or hostile. So it is neither in principle unfair, improper, nor unreasonable, for the civil servants in the Foreign Office to cling to their traditional assumption that theirs is a vocation set apart, to resist, in particular – as they still sternly do – the importation into their ranks of individuals qualified in the departments of the Home Civil Service, and to oppose, as they have on several occasions since the war, their own amalgamation with the Home Civil Service.

The critical question is the degree of exclusiveness and the degree of co-operation. Those Foreign Secretaries who have been most consistently happy at the Office have been those who have entered it with the greatest number of assumptions shared with its denizens – though there have been a few of massive personality and ability – like Curzon or Ernest Bevin – who have simply, on policy if not institutional questions, been able to impose themselves. The traditions of the Office, its methods of recruitment and administration, have been for so long extending their roots that they have been, as it sometimes seemed imperishably, successful in opposing change.

Bevin and Eden, Sir Val Duncan, Lord Plowden and the Central Policy Review Staff (the Think Tank) have all at various times since 1945 (the Think Tank most recently in 1977)[2] seen not dissimilar proposals for change run into the sand, in spite of enjoying a good deal of support in government circles, in Whitehall, and in sections of the press, where the Foreign Office has enjoyed – or endured – an increasing measure of disapproval over the years.

There has, indeed, been no significant internal change in the Foreign Office – save perhaps in the addition to it of the old Commonwealth Office – since the early years of this century when the first Lord Hardinge of Penshurst, Permanent Under-Secretary and, subsequently, Viceroy of India, introduced the Registry system – still, nearly eighty years later, the governing method by which documents are received, analysed and passed upwards within the Office. Hardinge had a passion for administrative efficiency. Such was needed after the long reign as Foreign Secretary of the Third Marquis of Salisbury who, after he became Prime Minister briefly in 1885 and again from 1886 to 1892 and 1895 to 1902, continued to preside over foreign affairs for most of that time. Salisbury was very probably the greatest of all British Foreign Secretaries, but he operated in effectively a much smaller world than his successors from the early years of this century. He had, none the less, manifold responsibilities, and a distinct penchant both for secrecy and for very personal diplomacy. His successor, Lord Lansdowne, from time to time suffered embarrassment upon finding that relevant Foreign Office files had remained at Salisbury's home, Hatfield House.

The remark about the smallness of Salisbury's world requires some explanation, since his periods of office coincided with the last great spell of British imperial power before the attenuated and painful contraction and decline of the twentieth century. But diplomacy then, it has to be remembered, was concentrated in far fewer effective areas: Europe (including Russia and the Near East) and, to a lesser extent, America and the Far East, especially Japan. India was separately administered, and fear about encroachments on her northern frontiers was very much a matter of relations with Russia, against whom

2. See Anthony Sampson, *The changing anatomy of Britain* (London, 1982), chapter fifteen.

countervailing pressures could be exerted through relations with Germany and Turkey. The *effective* world of diplomacy was, therefore, much smaller and narrower than it is today.

It has been a rhetorically effective device of critics of the Foreign Office to argue that its present bulk and present expensive outlay are unjustifiable because Britain has shed her Empire. The United Kingdom, said Duncan[3] in 1968, 'is now a major power of the second order.' In a vivid phrase he suggested that the country was like a man who, because of financial exigency, had to give up his Rolls-Royce for a smaller car. 'It is misleading and dangerous', the CPRS stated in 1977, 'to think that the United Kingdom can maintain its position in the world by keeping up appearances.' Such has been the tenor of most administrative criticism of the Office since at least the early 1960s. But the thrust of this criticism is misplaced. Quite apart from the higher real cost of everything nowadays, it is precisely because we live in so much more fissiparous a world than did Lord Salisbury that we require a diplomatic service more widely spread geographically and more variously trained as to its members. In the days of Empire the really crucial international decisions – including that for peace or war – were made in the councils of a very small number of states. The wealth of Britain could be earned in most of the more primitive parts of the Empire by the dedicated men of the Colonial Service with relatively little interference from the ambitions of the European powers with whom the Foreign Office traditionally dealt.

Thus, when it seemed at various moments during the late nineteenth and twentieth centuries that France and Britain might come to blows over territorial disputes in Africa the matter was resolved, and ultimately led to the alliance between the two powers which confronted Germany in 1914, in Europe, by their common realisation that Germany presented such a threat to both of them on the continent of Europe that they must not dissipate their individual strengths by quarrelling with one another in Africa. Today, on the other hand, it is vital for Britain as a member of the Western Alliance to be fully *au fait* with developments in Pakistan because of the potential threat poised to Western interests and oil lifelines in the Middle East by the incursion of the USSR into Afghanistan. (It is often the case, too, that a

3. Sampson, *op. cit.*

country the size of Pakistan in terms of power may enjoy a more intimate relationship with a middle-sized power like Britain, than with a suffocating protector of the might of the United States, ultimately more important to her survival though the more powerful country may be.) The relevant line of attack on the assumptions and philosophy of the Foreign Office's methods of conducting its business is not, therefore, on the principle of distinction it erects between the nature of real diplomacy – security, peace, war and alliances – and the more tawdry world of domestic politics. Rather, the grand question is whether in its own area as traditionally conceived the Foreign Office has been doing its job well. Has it effectively predicted events? Has it persuaded those who might be enemies to become friends? Has it correctly advised its political masters as to the line along which Britain's interests lie?

These matters will be discussed at greater length in due course. For the moment, however, it may be observed that, for instance, British diplomats were caught completely unawares by the disintegration of the Shah's government in Iran, even though its Middle Eastern expertise is greater, in terms of languages known and facts collected, than any other in the area. Again, in the long run-in to the Falklands war, although diplomats never wholly discounted, and sometimes even emphasised the danger of an Argentinian invasion, there was never any concerted presentation of the outline of serious danger to ministers. Again, Foreign Office advice on Rhodesia/Zimbabwe in 1979 and 1980 consistently encouraged the belief not only that Mr Mugabe would not win a free election, but also that he was a tool of the Soviet Union, apparently on the basis of his Marxist record. Apart from the fact that British diplomats (and many British politicians) simply preferred Mr Joshua Nkomo as the putative leader of an independent Zimbabwe, having had many dealings with him over the years, whereas Mr Mugabe was a relatively unknown factor, this electoral prediction seems to have been based on the belief that Bishop Muzorewa, hitherto an ally of Mr Ian Smith, being of the same Shona tribe as Mr Mugabe, would significantly cut into the latter's votes in Mashonaland, and thereafter be able to govern in alliance with Mr Nkomo's 'Ndebele. The electoral prediction was staggeringly wide of the mark, for Bishop Muzorewa was hard put to it even to retain his own seat in the new Parliament. Meanwhile, the prejudice seemingly based on fact and reliable judgement had led to Mr Mugabe being treated with scant respect during the Lancaster House constitutional conference in London, and the offence thus caused was repaired only by the adroit conduct of Lord Soames when he served in Salisbury as interim governor during the election period. It is fair, thus, to judge a self-consciously élite body by standards as high as its pretensions, and on that measure the Foreign Office's performance in recent years leaves a very great deal to be desired.

The Office's sense, however, of being, in Peter Jay's words, 'the custodians of the fundamental truths of British foreign policy . . .', suffered not a whit from such errors; the sense of a collective accuracy has never been as much as dented. Into the hallowed headquarters of this mighty institution Lord Carrington entered in 1979. He made a tour, and delighted everybody by the ease and affability of his manner. When he arrived in his own room – the largest, incidentally, of any Cabinet Minister, including the Prime Minister – he exclaimed, 'Lovely, lovely', though the appurtenances of that room have become somewhat threadbare over years of necessary government austerity. His sheer delight entranced his staff, as his pleasant informality of manner flattered them. This, after all, is where he had always wanted to be, where, indeed, he had craved to be. His pleasure was understandable, but it set a tone, and it indicated that the simple joy of *being* where he now was might exceed in its effect on his personality and attitudes any desire on his part to direct policy.

His reaction was altogether different from that of, say, Curzon, who entered the same room as Acting Foreign Secretary in 1919 (Arthur Balfour being in Paris for the Versailles Treaty negotiations) with the promise of the reversal of the Office. Curzon, of course, had been a brilliant Viceroy of India, but one so insistent on his own rights, and so high-handed in his relations with London, that one contemporary referred caustically to the fact that dealing with Curzon was less like dealing with a servant of the Crown than with a foreign power. Sir Harold Nicolson,[4] in what is probably the best book on British foreign policy written this century, *Curzon: the last phase*, describes the scene:

He then walked across the strip of once scarlet drugget

4. Harold Nicolson, *op. cit.*, pp. 44f.

towards the room of the Secretary of State. He paused for a moment on the threshold surveying the large Turkey carpet, the gay fireguard presented to Lord Salisbury by Li Hung Chang, the dimmed leather sofas and armchairs, the mahogany map-racks, the yellow standing desk in the corner. Three of the bleak though curtained windows looked northwards across the parade; three westwards towards St. James's Park. He walked to the windows and twitched the curtains into less lodging-house folds. His eyes travelled upwards to where the cast-iron beams of the ceiling had been disguised by Sir George Scott under an etrusco-byzantine ceiling.

'How ghastly!' he murmured, 'how positively ghastly'.

There is little doubt that Curzon, a man of almost impossibly wide learning and excellent taste, *did* find his quarters ghastly. But, as he revealed when, with gusto, he would retail this story in later years, there was method behind his manner. He was in a very tricky position. He by no means enjoyed the full confidence of the apparently all-powerful Prime Minister, David Lloyd George. He could not be sure he would command the full loyalty of the Office. The man he was replacing had been Prime Minister, was a scion of the House of Salisbury, was, still, probably the most powerful figure in the Tory – Curzon's own – party. Lloyd George was not a man noted for keeping his word, Balfour was a man inscrutable in his ambiguity (and was subsequently decisively to intervene in a contest between Curzon and Baldwin for the Prime Ministership, against Curzon). The Acting Secretary of State saw it as crucial to stamp himself on the Office, and did so in every area of its life.

I make the contrast between Curzon and Carrington principally to emphasise two entirely different approaches to the taking of high office under the Crown. It is, however, in one important sense, unfair. Lord Curzon, took up his task with deeply thought-out views on both the proper nature and the proper conduct of British foreign policy. These were, in many important respects, different from those of the Cabinet of which he was a member and the Prime Minister who had appointed him. To prevail, he needed an office which, if it could not be persuaded, could be bullied into giving him its support. Lord

Carrington, on the other hand, had no very strong views that differed from the collective views of his new Department. He had served as Secretary of State for Defence, and thus in terms of experience as well as interest had more than a nodding acquaintance with the requirements of foreign policy. Save, however, in his instinctive favouring of a harder line towards the Soviet Union than was current in British diplomatic circles – and the difference there was more a matter of emphasis than substance – he had nothing which he wanted to impose, and certainly no critique which he wanted to advance. In that, of course, his position was entirely different from that of the leader of his government, who had just come to No 10 Downing Street with a great many ideas which she wanted to impose on Whitehall. He could be forgiven, therefore, if on that May day he felt he had come home, and that whatever squalls the government would face in other areas, and however tricky and even dangerous were some of the problems with which he would himself have to deal, he would face no major problems with the machine which would serve him, and which he was only too willing to serve.

In his speech in the House of Lords on 25 January 1983 on the Franks Report it was, therefore, hardly surprising to find Carrington vigorously and even angrily defending the Office and its members against the frequently violent criticisms they had attracted since the outset of the Falklands crisis, saying:

> Those of us politicians who have worked with them know that there is no more dedicated or patriotic or skilful body of men in England; and I am overwhelmingly resentful of these unjustified criticisms, which are more revealing about the critic than about the criticised.

David Owen is rather less impressed:

> You have to know where the institutional prejudices exist and offset them by injecting some steel. There *is* a predominant insensitivity to Israel's legitimate security fears. There *is* a predominant Latin-American element that is too blind to the weaknesses of military juntas and right-wing governments.[5]

5. As quoted in the *Sunday Telegraph*.

From first to last, from May 1979 to April 1982, there is not one single instance, whether recorded or rumoured, of Carrington taking a different line on any matter of tactics or policy from that which emerged through the Foreign Office machine, save his refusal, in September 1981, to sanction a massive 'educational' programme to persuade the British public that the Falkland Islanders should *not* have the last say on the acceptance or otherwise of any deal negotiated between British and Argentinian diplomats. Even here there is no evidence that he disagreed with what his officials wanted in principle to do. He was merely aware of the impossibility of getting sufficient support for such a programme from the Cabinet and the Prime Minister.

It seems, on the common sense face of it, unlikely that any series of collections of human beings (I use the plural to emphasise the extraordinary consistency of Foreign Office attitudes over years) could be as correct as they are assumed to be. Of course, there have been major changes of front – for example, from being against British membership of the European Economic Community in its early days to being increasingly fanatically for that membership from the 1960s onwards. But the consistency of attitudes towards methods of making policy, and the consistency of attitudes towards the exact formulation of policy – the Middle East is a particularly good example – have been remarkable over the years. Again, common sense would suggest the unlikelihood of a Secretary of State in a determinedly reforming government finding himself immediately so at ease with a department that had been serving a government of very different complexion for the five previous years. There was, after all, no such case of transition in any other major department of state. Finally, it again offends against common sense to suggest that any single department could carry on as long as has the Foreign Office – since the Hardinge reforms – without any major internal change to meet changing external circumstances. None the less, that is what has happened.

There are many reasons why this phenomenon has been possible of achievement, for there is no doubt that it was an achievement sought continually and with dedication. With that Lord Falkland who gave his name to the South Atlantic islands successive generations of Foreign Office leaders could say, 'When it is not necessary to change, it is necessary not to change.' Such important changes as there were, which I will discuss in a later chapter, were in the field of policy, not administration, and were generated, almost invariably, internally, rather than as a result of political or governmental pressure. The reasons for this remarkable stability can be grouped under two heads – continuity of method of administration, and inculcation of a particular style. Each depended on the other.

The Scott building of which Lord Carrington was so enamoured was the architect's second try at devising a home – at the behest of Lord Palmerston – for the newly grandiloquent powerhouse for the international policy of a great Empire. The first, which Palmerston rejected, Scott thriftily kept in his files, and eventually caused to be erected as St Pancras railway station. The curious passer-by may therefore see at St Pancras what might have been at the Parliament end of Whitehall. Scott's conception had been, therefore, mock-Gothic, because that seemed to him to be most suitably imperial. Palmerston's conception was what the architect eventually provided, which was mock-Italian. It has space and solidity and a certain (now slightly shabby) grandeur, especially in its interior decoration. It does not, internally, glower with the dark panellings of the Victorian Cabinet Office further down Whitehall. Though hardly any more to be described as elegant inside it has none of the dinginess of the Department of Health and Social Security at Elephant and Castle. It has none of the pokiness of No 10 or No 11 Downing Street (the latter being the home of the Chancellor of the Exchequer). It has nothing of the soullessness of the new economic and administrative departments, like Environment. It has nothing of the grimness of Defence, also in Whitehall, nor of the primness of the Treasury in Great George Street. It is *sui generis*. There is no major political building in the country save the Houses of Parliament which is as remotely redolent to the same degree of history and confidence.

The major embassies abroad – even Sir Basil Spence's hideous modern confection in Rome – convey a very similar spirit, which, indeed, is often reflected in their internal workings. This is less one of ostentation or grandeur – though the Paris embassy, bought originally from Napoleon's sister, is one of the most opulent buildings in Paris – than of self-sufficiency. Peter Jay was originally sent to Washington by Dr Owen not for the political reasons frequently suggested at the time by a generally hostile press but, above all, to break down the isolation in which the Embassy's diplomatic staff of 600 were believed to live, functioning within their own community and socialising around the diplomatic circuit in preference to American society.

Here again, however, I believe that most of the more substantial critics of the Foreign Office – Plowden, Duncan and the CPRS – have missed the main point. Their arguments, in general, concentrated on three areas – lavish spending on the diplomatic service which Britain could not afford, failure to concentrate on producing the economic expertise required to assist the nation's export drive, and unduly selective recruitment of staff, principally from the public schools and Oxford and Cambridge. The argument against the existing selection process was that the type of recruit generally successful – especially in the administrative, or potentially high-flying grade – was, first, not representative of the country at large and, second, unlikely to possess the skills required to fit the modern diplomat for the modern world, mainly relevant languages and some skill in economics.

In its resistance to substantial cuts in expenditure the Foreign Office was almost wholly successful, at least until the deepening recession forced reductions on it. In the matter of what can only be called the acquisition of a salesman's skills there were some changes in some areas. Again, however, these were forced on the Office by circumstances, particularly that of Britain becoming a member of the European Economic Community. As regards recruitment the Office merely protested that it simply hired the applicants of greatest intelligence, and it was no part of their business to stipulate to schools and universities how aspiring diplomats could be trained. Moreover, so at least the private defence went, it was by no means necessary or logical that a diplomatic service should be representative of the nation as a whole. The vital question was whether or not it efficiently served the nation's interests. In this last point at least they were certainly right.

Where all these various criticisms – and there was at least some marginal validity to all of them – missed the point was in not defining clearly what the rôle of a diplomat is or should be. No doubt there was something to be said in criticism of the system of lax accounting and over-spending which characterised the activity of some embassies and which so shocked the young economists who made up Sir Kenneth Berrill's CPRS team. But the crucial test of a diplomat is how effective he is in the support of his government's policy, whether, when that policy is unclear he can help to clarify it, and whether, at all times, he presents a solid face on behalf of his government to the representatives of the nation to which he is accredited. The case against the Foreign Office is that, because of its exclusivity, its self-perpetuating nature and its isolation from the Home Civil Service it has less and less been able or willing to discharge this simple, but undoubtedly arduous duty.

Both the narrow band of selection in recruiting diplomats and the internal administrative structure of the Office are powerful aids in preserving intact the sense of the Foreign Office as an exclusive cadre. In no other department is it so difficult for a young man, however brilliant he may be, who is out of step with the general consensus and world view of his seniors, to cut his way through opposition to the top, perhaps by gaining the attention of his political masters. As Mrs Thatcher showed in 1982 by a reshuffle of top jobs in the Home Civil Service which brought her own Private Secretary to the Permanent Under Secretaryship of the Ministry of Defence and, in general, by-passed the system of 'Buggins's turn' which characterises most Civil Service promotion, it is possible for a determined politician from time to time to cut through inertia. But the Foreign Office remained untouched by her moves, and it is not yet clear whether she has the will – or whether her own foreign policy staff at No 10 Downing Street, headed for a time by Sir Anthony Parsons, one of the few diplomats for whom she has a high regard, has the power – to effect great changes in this regard. What is beyond doubt is that the Prime Minister had come to the conclusion, at the end of Lord Carrington's term, that the Office was opposed to certain important aspects of and emphases in her own foreign policy. It also seems, however, that rather than embark on any serious restructuring of the Office itself, she prefers simply to make her own policy directly to other heads of government. This is a situation with which the Foreign Office has had to cope more than once in this century, and it is clearly set for a struggle.

Before analysing the pros and cons of this emerging clash of author-ity in foreign policy between a Prime Minister and the Foreign Office, three things should be borne in mind. First, there is nothing new about such divisions. On several occasions in this century the clash was far more virulent than it was at the beginning of the Falkland crisis, or even than it is now. Sometimes the Foreign Office was victorious – partly because it possesses a longer institutional consistency than the

Prime Minister's office, partly because it has more resources – sometimes No 10 was. The acid test here is which side can can hold on longer, until events or habit settle the country on a changed course. Second, the techniques of modern communications, from hotline to supersonic air transport, give the leader of any government a greater opportunity than ever before for the successful making of foreign policy, through negotiating directly with other leaders. This fact has constituted the single greatest difficulty faced by the Foreign Office in retaining a grip on the web of international relations. Third, the Foreign Office is at its most powerful when it is able to work in complete harmony with the Foreign Secretary, or he with it. This was the situation that prevailed during the term of office of Lord Carrington. Given that he was also a senior Conservative Party statesman – in a way which Dr Owen was not in the Labour Party – and that he was thought by her to be important in party terms to the consolidation of her authority in the early years of government it meant that he could, if not quell, at least quieten the suspicions the Prime Minister harboured about his department. (The one exception to this general experience, before the outbreak of the Falkland crisis, was the series of EEC summits on the question of Britain's contribution to the Community budget which began in 1979, shortly after she was elected.)

In the early days of the Falkland crisis the critics – usually harsh in the extreme, and including myself – emphasised two occasionally contradictory judgements about the conduct of the Foreign Office in the years, but more particularly the months, preceding the outbreak of armed conflict. The first was on the Office's incompetence. Were they so hopeless at their jobs, it was asked, that they could not see, even up to the witching hour, what was going to happen, did not, perhaps, read the Argentinian newspapers, even though Embassy officials in Buenos Aires were fully aware of the fact that Señor Iglesias Rouca of *La Prensa*, author of frequent predictions of invasion, had highly reliable sources in the Argentinian defence establishment? (The Franks Commission's report confirms this high appreciation of Señor Rouca's fact-finding ability.) In the caustic words of one journalist, 'Perhaps they were too busy trying to winkle secret information out of Argie politicians to read the local papers.'

The second judgement was what amounted to a finding of

conspiracy. All along, so the argument ran, the Foreign Office – viewed as a collective intelligence – was determined that the Islands should be handed back to Argentina as soon as domestic British political conditions would permit, *or could be made to permit*. The significance of this last phrase is demonstrated in Lord Franks' account[6] of a recommendation to Carrington to suggest to the Defence Committee (of the Cabinet) 'a much more public and active campaign to educate Islander and British public opinion'. The stumbling block as the Foreign Office saw it, was the insistence (made with, as I have mentioned, varying degrees of emphasis) by successive governments that sovereignty would not be handed to Argentina without the consent of the Islanders. The phrase I have just quoted meant, therefore, persuading the Islanders and the British to downgrade the issue of British sovereignty, since no amount of persuasion could induce Argentinian governments to downgrade *their* claims.

Carrington vetoed any idea of his supporting this course of action. In doing so he was acting quite properly, both on grounds of principle and realism. The policy had been reiterated so often and by so many ministers of both parties that it had to be regarded as a bedrock. Moreover, it would be unrealistic to imagine, even if ministers were unscrupulous enough surreptitiously to go back on earlier commitments (and a programme of 'education' clearly did not visualise open and honest argument for a willingness in principle to abandon sovereignty, but a process of fudging the question), that party, parliamentary or public opinion would fail to see through the gossamer-thin cloak of pretence.

It is instructive to note, however, that so patently fraudulent a course should have been advocated with such little evident concern about its fraudulence. It was a case, put simply, of a department – wrongly, as it happened on this occasion – being confident enough of the support of its minister for its views, assuming a readiness on his part to join with them in persuading his Cabinet colleagues to pull the wool over the eyes of the electorate. It strongly supports the second contention of the critics of the Foreign Office, and buttresses some of the analysis in a striking report on the Foreign Office which appeared

6. *Falkland Islands Review: report of a committee of Privy Counsellors* (Cmnd. 8787, 1983).

before the Franks report was published, on 27 November 1982. *The Economist* then said:

> From Lord Chalfont in the 1960s and Mr. Nicholas Ridley and Mr. Richard Luce in 1981–2, ministers recall their Falklands parliamentary question times as the worst moments of their foreign office careers. Officials made no attempt to learn in advance the lessons of previous failures or guard them against the hostility and suspicion they were sure to encounter. One minister commented afterwards, 'It was as if they took a delight in watching us make the same mistakes over again.' What is surprising is that so many were prepared to be led thus to the slaughter (there have been seven Falklands ministers since 1965). As it was, foreign observers were astonished to see three ministers forced into resignation after the Argentine invasion, while all the permanent officials responsible remained at their desks.

The worst that happened, indeed, was that Sir Michael Palliser, the Permanent Under-Secretary in the period leading up to the crisis, did not receive the customary peerage immediately on his retirement.

It is certainly astonishing that Lord Franks and his colleagues had no animadversions to make upon so blatantly devious a course of action. It issued, of course, out of a sense of despair at an inability to square the circle of negotiations with the Argentinians, the attempts to do which are amply chronicled by Franks. The problem was that, with both sides immovable on sovereignty, and the Argentinian tolerance over time increasingly limited, there were only two options. The first was to garrison the Islands in sufficient strength to guard against an Argentinian incursion, the second to concede the principle of sovereignty and devise something such as the leaseback formula, whereby Argentinian sovereignty was conceded, but she leased the territory back to Britain for a specified period. Concession or leaseback were the courses favoured by the Foreign Office, the first option – on Franks's evidence – being ruled out on grounds of cost or distortion of the defence effort.

But the ruling out, on the evidence presented by Franks, was arbitrary, on the part of politicians and diplomats alike, but particularly the latter. In vain we search the pages of *Falkland Islands Review* for discussion of any paper seeking to describe and cost what would be needed to defend the Islands by force of arms. The assumption is, simply, that the cost would be vast. Yet, of course, military cost is relative not only to the nation undertaking it, but to the question of what would be required to deter the rival feared. It would be open to officials to argue their opinion that the visualised cost would be bearable or unbearable. It was dereliction of duty simply not to attempt the exercise. That dereliction can be put down either to incompetence or to a hypocritical defence of a position already decided upon. For politicians not to have demanded the production of such a paper, which could then have been examined by defence experts, was most certainly incompetent. In any event, assuming from the long experience of frustrating negotiations with Argentinian governments – from 1965 onwards – that there might ultimately be a stark choice between surrender and fight – and there was that assumption – the politicians should have been faced clearly with an account of their choices at an early stage. That they were not, given *The Economist* report of the eternal inadequacy of service to ministers responsible for the Falklands from 1965 onwards, convinces me that there was, throughout, an Office policy of nudging ministers at whatever opportunity arose towards the policy the Office favoured. And such a course is, of course, constitutionally quite improper.

As the war began, but perhaps most particularly when it was over, such considerations as these were brought to the attention of the Prime Minister. All her hitherto partly suppressed, and certainly inadequately articulated suspicions of the Foreign Office boiled over. Threatening noises emanated from No 10 Downing Street. She and her staff had already decided on one of the principal recommendations that was to emerge from the Franks Commission – that the coveted post of Chairman of the Joint Intelligence Committee should be taken from the Office and given to a trusted independent. The Office were worried: their best protector, Carrington, had gone, and Francis Pym, though willing to break a lance for them, enjoyed doubtful standing in the Party and none with the Prime Minister. There is no doubt that she, and those closest to her, were in a mood of exceptional anger. Whether supportive of her or not, most of the press and other media did share one general opinion, that the depth of the conflict was unprecedented.

It is, in fact, mild compared to what has gone before it. Indeed, it is only by understanding the length of this recurring conflict and its character that one can begin to see a way forward to a reform of the government machine – and the Foreign Office – which might meet the requirements of the hour.

Of all ministers of the Crown the two most nearly independent of the Prime Minister are the Foreign Secretary and the Chancellor of the Exchequer. The nature of much of the Chancellor's business is to a degree highly technical. Once a broad strategy is agreed in Cabinet – over which a forceful Prime Minister will undoubtedly exercise much sway – its implementation, especially when, towards the end of a given calendar year, the Chancellor and his advisers retreat into purdah to work out the technical implications of that strategy, becomes virtually unsupervisable. The longer a Chancellor serves, moreover, the greater the amount of information virtually unintelligible to outsiders becomes available to him, and the more readily he can, in effect, veto bold or desperate new proposals from the Prime Minister, even though the Prime Minister enjoys the title of First Lord of the Treasury.

Initiatives in foreign policy are more readily undertaken by a Prime Minister, not least because of the modern facility in communications which, as I mentioned earlier, the holder of that office enjoys. But the sustaining, the working out, of such initiatives are more often than not governed by the enthusiasm (or lack of it) which the Foreign Office and its head feel. If a problem in foreign policy has a definite and foreseeable end then the enthusiasm or commitment of the Prime Minister, whether in agreement with the Foreign Office or not, can ensure that it is seen through to its end. Thus, though the Foreign Office was exceptionally supportive of Edward Heath's bid to bring Britain into the Common Market, it is fair to say that it was Heath's direct approach to President Pompidou – which involved a change of negotiating tactics – which brought about the desired end. But when the matter was one – in 1979 and 1980 – of reducing Britain's budgetary commitment to the Community, the Prime Minister and the Foreign Office had different ends as well as tactics. She was determined at all costs to secure a massive proportion of the sum she named. They were merely willing to accept a great deal less, a cosmetic sum, in fact. They regarded that acceptance as a fundamental strategic necessity. She overrode them and won, because she handled most of the details herself, and directly with other heads of government. But such an effort, on such a major issue, can be sustained by a Prime Minister for only a brief period, because a Prime Minister has a great many other matters to attend to, and cannot for long concentrate on only one subject.

In its different guises and dimensions the struggle between the Foreign Office – sometimes but not always in the company of the Foreign Secretary – and the Prime Minister – sometimes but not always supported by the rest of the Cabinet – has been going on throughout this century. Of course, in earlier periods of history the King made one policy and his ministers another. Or factions within a ministry advocated different policies abroad. But since the structure of British government settled down into something like its present form the particular struggle which will continue to be dramatic in the post-Falklands period has emerged in one guise or another.

The Liberal government elected in 1906 entered office before the election itself. Sir Edward Grey, its Foreign Secretary, failed to inform his Cabinet colleagues, including the Prime Minister, Sir Henry Campbell-Bannerman, of the fact that his Conservative predecessor, Lord Lansdowne, had been on the verge of concluding a secret military agreement with France against Germany. He subsequently explained – when all this was discovered after the war – that the exigencies of an election campaign made consultation impossible. Lord Loreburn, however, the Liberal Lord Chancellor who resigned on Britain's declaration of war in 1914, subsequently demonstrated that consultation would have been easy.

As the years of Liberal government went on, Grey and the Foreign Office worked to cement Anglo-French ties. Full Cabinet consultation was undesirable, since it was doubtful whether a majority could be obtained for the policy. Even if a majority could be obtained there would be sufficient resignations to imperil the policy, if not the government. In 1911 something of what had been going on reached the ears of potential dissenters. Grey was forced to write an ambiguous letter to his French opposite number which satisfied both sides; but he accompanied it with private assurances which more than satisfied the French, and which were of a character which led Britain into war in 1914. Bertie, the British Ambassador in France, doubted both the wisdom of the strategy and the propriety of Grey's conduct. He was told to keep silence, and did so, thus demonstrating the extraordinary command the Foreign Secretary had over the behaviour of his civil servants. In the pre-war debate in 1914 – when the House of Commons had to decide whether or not Britain would go to war, Grey, by omitting parts of his letters to France, lied to the House. When he was cross-examined by G. P. Gooch and Harold Temperley on his conduct during their preparation of the multi-volume *Documents on the Origins of the War*[7] he offered a series of increasingly improbable explanations for his conduct, ranging from the absurd suggestion that the omitted passages were of no importance to the vainglorious one that he *had* read the passages, but that the applause was so great that the *Hansard* writer had not heard him.

I have already described Curzon's determination to impose himself on the Foreign Office because he foresaw the difficulties he would have in asserting his authority against that of Lloyd George in post-war reconstruction. For four years Curzon was virtually impotent, and saw with despair the increasing – and increasingly inconsistent – emergence of a foreign policy alternative to his own from No 10 Downing Street, a policy the details of which were handled by those serving in the famous 'garden suburb' (the prefabs that Lloyd George had had erected) in the garden of Downing Street. On the Near East, on relations with Russia, and in general on relations between the old allies and their former German enemy, Lloyd George and his Foreign Secretary were regularly and increasingly at odds. But Curzon's reluctance to resign (he had done so once before, and spent ten years in the wilderness as a consequence) and Lloyd George's repeated asseverations of personal warmth towards the Foreign Secretary ensured that the issue of authority would not be readily resolved. It was not until Lloyd George's successors, Bonar Law and Baldwin, gave Curzon a virtually free hand in foreign policy that he was able to apply the principles, policies and methods that he himself favoured, and restore the British reputation that Lloyd George had left, broken, in the dust. The opposition of Anthony Eden, when Foreign Secretary in the 1930s, to the policy of appeasement of Germany and Italy favoured by the Prime Minister, Neville Chamberlain, is well known, though it was

7. See G. P. Gooch and Harold Temperley (eds.), *British documents on the origins of the war 1898–1914* (London, 1926–38).

not as unqualified as Eden's admireres have insisted. The fissure that opened between Eden and Chamberlain was, however, undoubtedly great, and on a matter of paramount importance not merely to the prosperity or the future, but the very existence of the country. Chamberlain increasingly drew the making of policy to himself and his personal adviser, Sir Horace Wilson. When Eden resigned and Sir Robert Vansittart, the resolutely anti-appeasement Permanent Under-Secretary at the Foreign Office, was moved aside to the meaningless post of Special Adviser to the government, the Office was, as has rarely happened, divided. It did not matter. Chamberlain now had the matter wholly in his own hands, and time was short.

In 1940, as the ramparts of France crumbled, the Foreign Secretary, Lord Halifax, and the Office, came to the conclusion that a fresh effort at an agreement with Germany should be made through Mussolini. Feelers were put out in Scandinavia, and in the United States British diplomats spoke to this effect, in spite of the absolutely categorical character of the stated policy of the Churchill government. Churchill himself, not long, after all, in power, felt impelled to adjourn that meeting of the War Cabinet at which Halifax raised the matter and sustained it stubbornly. Having, however, reassured himself of the redoubtable support of Attlee, of the junior ministers, and of the Conservative Party in Parliament, he had little difficulty in crushing Halifax. This incident is not as striking an example as the others I have adduced in this section. In wartime, all things are different, and it is proper that the central direction of foreign policy should lie in the hands of the Prime Minister. None the less, it is striking that a man of such unbounded self-confidence and sense of destiny as Churchill should have felt compelled, at the very hour which he had singled out as his own, to manoeuvre, once he had locked horns with his Foreign Secretary.

The events leading to the invasion of Egypt in 1956 by Britain, France and Israel are too fresh in the memory to need more than the briefest adumbration here. For all that he wanted Nasser's head, and to an unbalanced degree, Sir Anthony Eden found it hard indeed to take the decision for war, and prevaricated endlessly on the road to that decision. Historians, political scientists and even politicians are still divided on whether it was right or wrong. On one thing all are, however, agreed, that the execution of the policy, and especially the delays in that execution, political and military, were disastrous. It is certainly the case that Eden's prevarication weakened both his case and his power. But it has to be remembered that he was beset on all sides by doubters. The Foreign Secretary, Selwyn Lloyd, as he recorded in the book he wrote on the subject before his death,[8] had his own doubts, which were resolutely and repeatedly reinforced by virtually the whole strength of the Foreign Office. French and Israeli participants in the secret talks which led to the Suez assault remarked to one another (and some recorded in their memoirs) how evident was the division in British ranks, and how distasteful the Foreign Office found the whole idea. The same impression was received from British diplomats around the world, most notably – and most importantly – in Washington. Eden himself had been twice Foreign Secretary. He had longed for that job fully as much as, in later years, Peter Carrington had, and he had yearned for it with a hunger that is beyond Carrington's much more measured and balanced personality. The evidence suggests that the often bitter opposition of his old department contributed not a little to the nervous havering that so imperilled his whole plan.

There is, in a comparison between the period leading up to the Suez invasion and the period leading up to the first action of the Task Force in the Falklands, a particular and significant point of propriety to be repeated and emphasised.

It was clear from the moment that President Nasser announced the nationalisation of the Suez Canal that the British and French governments (and other governments, too, but the British and French were the most important, since nobody else would consider military action) had a choice between negotiation and force. Negotiation could be either on the terms of a face-saving surrender to Egypt or aimed towards one of the very many internationally approved formulae which were canvassed in the agonising weeks before Israel launched the attack in Sinai which brought in its train, as was planned, action by Britain and France. As time scurried by it was clear that President Nasser held all the negotiating cards, and that the only choice was between surrender and war. In spite of the fact that Her Majesty's Government had repeatedly asserted that, if the choice was posed in

8. Selwyn Lloyd, *Suez 1956* (London, 1978)

such stark terms they would choose war, Her Majesty's Foreign Office continued to argue for and to work for surrender.

In the months – even in the years – leading to the conflict in the South Atlantic, as I have already described, British governments took a similar position on the Falklands. A surrender of sovereignty without the consent of the Islanders – which, as the Argentinians correctly saw, was unlikely to be forthcoming except in an extremely distant and probably unimaginable future – was unacceptable, though the Argentinians were more than welcome to try persuasion by the fostering of ever closer links between mainland and Islands. If necessary, however – that is, if violent Argentinian action made it necessary – the British government of the day would fight. Never mind that both the Argentinians and outside commentators who saw the logistical difficulties involved in a successful response to an Argentinian thrust doubted whether any British government would keep that pledge. It was the duty of British diplomats having been told that this was the policy of the government, and whatever their private reservations, to make it crystal clear to Argentinian governments and Argentinian opinions that this was the policy.

Instead, our diplomats had reservations about the policy, which resulted in a failure to spell out, and have tested, opinions as to the likely relative cost of defence to surrender. They led to imbalance of judgement in a failure, when reporting back to the Foreign Secretary and the Cabinet, to take seriously the oft-repeated, oft-declared statements of Argentinian intentions. And they led to a failure to discharge duty with clarity and force in informing the Argentinians of what the policy was. Every shred of evidence that we have from every available Argentinian source demonstrates that the representatives of British diplomacy – and of British government – never got that simple point, the duty of making which ineluctably flowed from the enunciation of the policy devolved on any official or politician who spoke to an Argentinian, whether officially or privately. But, of course, in Carrington's words, 'It *can't* come to that.' Perhaps he expressed the best, if most bleak judgement on the calibre of his stewardship when, discussing his resignation with Robert Kee on BBC's *Panorama* programme on the night he resigned, he said, 'What I think was – and this is why I felt it right to resign – I think that on what we knew, the judgements that I made as Foreign Secretary were right. But it turned out that they were wrong . . .'

There was a great deal more wrong than judgements. But wrong judgements, not merely of Argentinian intentions, but of British reactions, were close to the heart of the matter. There was also the matter of political (or even moral) judgement. Few indeed would argue that a constitutional impropriety is *never* permissible, even if it serves a great national end. The few who heard Grey in the House of Commons in 1914, and knew that he was lying, were the true believers in his policy, those who thought it a vital national interest to go to war with Germany on the utterly spurious pretence that we were acting in support of the sanctity of an early nineteenth-century treaty to defend the territorial integrity of Belgium. Few, indeed, of the many who opposed with profound bitterness Eden's Suez policy would readily find it in themselves to condemn on grounds of propriety the many diplomats who sought to undermine him.

The historian of the origins of the First World War, however, the historian of the 1920s, the historian of 1940, or the historian of 1956 can readily take a more detached view of matters than can the political writer (or politician) considering the events that took place in 1982. The *immediate* effects of what was left undone, and done, in the first half of 1982, have a tangible effect on the life of politics today, and will have a tangible effect on the life of politics in the nation for years to come. The effect of anything that happened between 1914 and 1956, considered in terms of the conflict between the Foreign Office and the Prime Minister of the day, is necessarily understood, or felt, to be much more remote. Most thinking citizens accept that they are a part of their country's – and their society's – historical evolution, but it is what happened last year, or five years ago, that seems to most of us more immediately relevant.

Thus, the Falklands crisis, and the manner in which it has been so far resolved, has a distinct and immediate bearing on the length, durability and character of Mrs Thatcher's contribution to, and rôle in, British public life. If what has been called the 'Falklands factor' contributes to her retaining a major influence on the whole of British politics for some time to come, then her reaction to the Argentinian invasion will be seen as not merely a turning-point in her own fortunes, but possibly as a turning-point in British politics as a whole. For these reasons – since it is so readily understood that the current profound difference between her and the Foreign Office reached its point of explosion because of that Office's conduct in relation to the Islands – politicians and commentators alike tend to forget the historical, one might say the endemic, if recurring nature of the conflict between the Foreign Office and Downing Street. It has been dramatic between Mrs Thatcher and the Office over which Lord Carrington presided, partly because events in the South Atlantic so decreed it, but partly because Britain had, in 1982, a Prime Minister with an instinct for the dramatic, against whom were ranged all the instincts for caution of her entire foreign policy establishment.

It should not be imagined, however, that no more than vague instincts of suspicion guided the Prime Minister in her – as I described it earlier – half-articulated attitude to the Foreign Office, and the methods as well as the policies it preferred, though no profound historical understanding of the nature of the problem was there either. In 1977 she received from the foreign policy adviser she probably most trusts a memorandum advising her on (in the writer's view) the proper course her public campaign of warning against the character and ambitions of the Soviet Union should take. In his covering letter he wrote:

> Nor are all Conservatives, either, immune from comfortable delusions, in the absence of adequate guidance. And among them are people who think they understand foreign affairs, *without having really made the intellectual and imaginative effort required. What is more, in the Foreign Office, there is a tendency to that* deformation professionelle *which regards negotiation, with the search for suitable concession, as desirable in itself and more central to fruitful relations than a grasp of the essentials.*

All the emphases in the passage I have just quoted were added by the Prime Minister.

The distaste for compromise and the need for action are the most common Prime Ministerial desires in foreign policy. Certainly there have been Prime Ministers in our history – Stanley Baldwin was probably the most prominent – who had no marked desire for action anyway, and no interest whatsoever in foreign affairs. But Baldwin was, in this as in many other respects, rare. There is no equivalent, and almost necessary preference on the part of a diplomat – or most foreign ministers – for inaction, as there is a Prime Ministerial preference for action. But, on the part of the British Diplomatic Service at least, there is, once a policy they find agreeable is established, very much a preference for endless negotiation at almost whatever cost, rather than for decision, at cost, whether political or military.

It is, of course, quite proper that a diplomat should seek to achieve his country's ends through negotiation: that is what he is paid for. As Talleyrand, a great foreign minister under French régimes of very different character, once observed, the rule of a diplomat should be *'pas trop de zèle'*. It is quite another thing to use lack of zeal – inanition – in the service of one policy and against another. Since in the early and middle 1960s the Foreign Office had become convinced that the entire thrust of British foreign policy should be concentrated in Europe, and in our membership of the EEC, it was very understandable that the members of the Office charged with ineffably tedious discussions with a South American government on the question of sovereignty over a thinly populated group of – on the face of it – inhospitable islands should seek to close the problem down by concession. After all, whatever their political masters were saying for public consumption in regard to the Islanders making the final decision on the matter of any cession of sovereignty, none of the politicians had been very energetic in pressing on with development of the Islands.

Thus, I believe, the Foreign Office read the situation. They read it with pleasure, as did Carrington. After all, as he said to the Royal Institute of International Affairs on 22 February 1980, the days of establishing Western – that is to say NATO – overseas bases were over. Large-scale military operations by Western powers were, he said, likewise, at an end. And, in that dismissive and humorous, but none the less crude way he has he added, 'The time for that kind of thing is past.' For just under thirty years it was past, and it issued then in turmoil in a nation, and for a nation.

7. THE RECORD

The primary task of the policy-maker is to articulate the country's external interests and order them in some scheme of relative importance. The articulation and ordering of interests must be continually changing through time, but a rough and ready pattern in the case of most states might follow the following lines: . . . There follows the difficult concept of independence, meaning the relative freedom of a country from interference in what it regards as its internal affairs, and some degree of power to express and implement an independent viewpoint on external affairs. It may be that the concept of sovereign independence no longer fits the facts of an independent twentieth century world. Nations none the less have an impression of their independence . . .

F. S. Northedge, *The Foreign Policies of the Powers*
(London, 1968).

Despite the aura of glamour that so often attaches itself to the business of diplomacy, opportunities for striking initiatives in foreign policy, such as may lead to a change in the constellation of international affairs, rarely present themselves to a medium-sized power. 'Very occasionally', writes David Vital in *The Making of British Foreign Policy*[1], 'a great political decision is taken – one which appears to the historian, in retrospect, as an event of unusual importance because a great series of consequences can be shown to follow or lead off from it.'

Vital believes that the only such decision made by successive British governments during the post-war period was that to seek membership of the Common Market. That decision was taken during the period of office of the Macmillan government and as the Prime Minister moved towards it he was already embarking headlong on the process of dismantling the British Empire in Africa. When Mrs Thatcher came to office in 1979 entry to the Common Market had been achieved, though the new system of relationships could hardly be regarded as a

1. David Vital, *The Making of British Foreign Policy* (London, 1968).

fully satisfactory one. At the same time the African Empire had ceased to exist, save for the intractable problem of Rhodesia which had, in 1965, declared unilateral independence from Britain, thus isolating herself from the mainstream of world politics, and settled down to a long and costly guerrilla war with dissident black forces. The new Conservative government remained pledged – to the United Nations and to the Commonwealth – to return the country to legality and to create a system of government allowing of black majority rule.

This pledge had been given by former Conservative and Labour governments. Despite many squabbles, and a great number of tactical differences, it had been held to both by Harold Wilson and by Edward Heath, but by the middle of 1979 the situation, so far as London was concerned, was complicated by three factors, two of long-standing, one much more recent. In the first place Wilson had from the beginning eschewed the use of force to bring the Smith government to heel, though there were voices on the left of British politics which cried out for stern measures. Rather, he embarked on a policy of imposing economic sanctions. There can hardly be much doubt that, given the bush war, and in spite of the frequently half-hearted respect for sanctions shown by the international community, the Salisbury government was in some real difficulty by the end of 1978. Smith and his ministers, moreover, were not helped by the fact that the South African government – their one friend in the world – were less than consistent or full-hearted in the support they offered, there being significant sections of South African opinion which took the view that independent Rhodesia was a constant and dangerous drain on South African resources, and that Pretoria's interests might be better served by a weak black government, such as has since been established. In any event, whatever might have been the possibilities in 1965, there could be no question of resolving the situation in 1979 through a resort to arms by Britain.

Mrs Thatcher, moreover, was troubled by an internal party problem of long duration regarding this question.

From even before UDI a moderately large, if not exactly politically powerful section of the right wing of the Conservative party had espoused the cause of Ian Smith and the white settlers whose chief he was. At various times during intermittent and unsuccessful exchanges between London and Salisbury, this section had urged the recognition of the Smith government, given more or less cosmetic concessions on its part. It was widely and correctly assumed that Mrs Thatcher had come to the leadership of the party with the practically undivided support of the right: it was presumed, therefore, that she had debts to pay. Since between 1975 and 1979 such public utterances as she had made on foreign policy had been confined mainly to the Soviet threat and the state of the Western Alliance, it was not known very clearly what her views on Africa were or if, indeed, she had any. It was generally presumed that she would accept a settlement which would fall short of handing the government of Rhodesia over to the Patriotic Front, the two leaders of whose separate, and often conflicting, wings, were Joshua Nkomo and Robert Mugabe.[2] They were guerrillas – terrorists, many said – and the new Prime Minister seemed not the type to bend to terror. She seemed untouched by the sentimental attachment, not only of the Labour Party, but of Harold Macmillan's intellectual heirs in the Conservative Party, to black causes in Africa. Moreover, an opportunity was at hand for what some Foreign Office officials called 'the second-class solution'.

Throughout 1978 the war in Rhodesia had increasingly taken on the character of a bloody slog. Rhodesia's was a siege economy, and if miracles of improvisation had kept it going, it was none the less beginning to crack. Over the years Ian Smith had made various attempts to come to diplomatic terms with Joshua Nkomo. Since Nkomo had responded to his overtures, rifts had appeared in the Patriotic Front. However, none of the various exchanges – some of them under the patronage of President Kenneth Kaunda of Zambia, Nkomo's chief African supporter – had borne fruit and Smith turned his attention to other potential black leaders within Rhodesia itself, principal among them Bishop Abel Muzorewa – like Mugabe, from the Shona tribe – and Ndabininge Sithole. By the end of 1978 a black-fronted government was ready in Salisbury, and in April 1979, following a general election, Muzorewa, however hedged about by Smith and his supporters, became Prime Minister of Rhodesia. This was the third major factor facing Mrs Thatcher. No previous British Prime Minister had faced such a problem, and it measurably increased the pressure on her from the Conservative right simply to recognise the

2. David Smith and Colin Simpson (with Ian Davies), *Mugabe* (London, 1981).

Bishop's government, lift sanctions and resume ordinary relations with a new Rhodesia. Fear that she might do so was rampant in the Patriotic Front, and suspicion of how the British Prime Minister would behave was rank. As Sally – Mrs Robert – Mugabe wrote to a friend, 'The political situation in Zimbabwe is unstable as usual. But this time it seems that lady Thatcher's government are bent on doing something out of the ordinary, by lifting sanctions and recognising an illegal régime. What does lady Thatcher want to prove, that she is a racist? I expect she is . . .'

Immediately on her accession to office, therefore, Mrs Thatcher, and her first Foreign Secretary, faced one of those critical moments in international politics mentioned at the beginning of this chapter. A recognition of Bishop Muzorewa would endanger the very existence of the Commonwealth. Nor was it only the black African – and probably Asian – members who would be offended. So would Australia where the Prime Minister, Malcolm Fraser, though a hard conservative in matters of domestic policy, was an out-and-out liberal in African affairs, implacably opposed to South Africa, and with his face set against any recognition of the *status quo* in Rhodesia.

On the other hand, there was much to be said for cutting the painter. The Conservative right wished for recognition of Rhodesia largely as a matter of sentiment and principle. But, within the Foreign Office in particular, a pragmatic school of thought had been emerging, with quite other considerations in mind.

Any agreed settlement, it was said, would be virtually impossible to achieve. Harold Macmillan (before UDI), Harold Wilson, Edward Heath and Alec Douglas-Home had all tried hard and failed: it was known to be one of Ian Smith's favourite themes, expressed in humorous monologues, that he had found it easy to shrug off British Prime Ministers; he dwelt on their numbers with relish. Then, the bright hopes of 1972, when the Treaty of Brussels had seen British entry into the EEC, had not been fulfilled. Hard work and unremitting application on Britain's part would be required if the whole experiment of membership was not going to collapse. This, ran the argument, was what the Foreign Secretary should be concentrating on; any African involvement would demand too much of his time and energy. (This prediction was correct. Rhodesia was the predominant concern of Carrington until the end of the year.) On the basis of her own statements the Prime Minister was seen to be concerned above all in foreign affairs with East–West relations. Could she afford to become bogged down in an African morass, given that she would also have to shoulder the burden of a major programme of radical domestic reform?

Of all these considerations the difficulty of achieving an agreed settlement weighed most with Carrington. He was profoundly depressed and pessimistic, said one of his civil servants. 'He did not see how he could succeed, but he could not bring himself firmly to advocate recognition either.'

On all the evidence, the Prime Minister appears initially to have had no settled views, though there was perhaps a slight inclination towards Muzorewa. On her own initiative she had sent Lord Boyd of Merton – as Alan Lennox-Boyd he had been Colonial Secretary in the Macmillan government – to observe the Rhodesian elections of April. Given, he reported, that there was a bush war going on, and that the Patriotic Front had succeeded in preventing many rural voters from going to the polls, the election had been as free and fair as anybody could reasonably have expected. On the other hand, the hope of Smith and Muzorewa that the very existence of a black government would bring many of the guerillas out from the jungle had been severely disappointed.

There was one other important consideration. Mrs Thatcher's first appearance on an international stage as Prime Minister would be at the Commonwealth Prime Ministers' conference in Lusaka in August. The Queen would be present, and Her Majesty was known to set great store by the preservation of Commonwealth links. Rhodesia would be certain to be top of the Lusaka agenda and, as I learned when I flew out to Lusaka shortly after the British election to see President Kaunda, the African leaders at least would arrive there imbued with the fiercest hostility to Mrs Thatcher and the most profound suspicion of her intentions.

In June the Prime Minister visited Australia. In the course of a press conference there she reiterated a commitment in the Conservative manifesto to the effect that, if the Muzorewa government could be shown to meet certain ambivalently defined standards of decency, recognition would follow. She also repeated a view strongly held on the right – that the new House of Commons would not, as required annually, renew sanctions on Rhodesia. All this was taken to mean that she was preparing the way for recognition.

As time marched towards Lusaka she was inundated by advice from all quarters. It would be entirely wrong to say, as so many writers have since suggested, that Carrington through tireless advocacy persuaded her to abandon the idea of recognition. But he was certainly more alive than she was – if uneasily so – to the dangerous international consequences of lifting sanctions. She attended a number of meetings at the Foreign Office where, as she put it after one of them, in a contemptuous tone of voice, 'all that was advocated was a do-nothing policy'. A new idea was now emerging which was, in fact, an old idea revived, that Britain should internationalise the Rhodesian problem by handing it over to the United Nations, thereafter conducting herself as a loyal member of that organisation, but disclaiming any responsibility for the colony. She dismissed this out of hand.

'Peter's not being much help, is he?,' she asked after one meeting with her Foreign Secretary. At that meeting – as at others – he did not fail to stress the uproar and upheaval that would follow any lifting of sanctions, but on the other hand he could see no way ahead either. One member of her political Private Office (someone, that is, whose salary was paid by the Party) expressed bitterness at what he took to be the debilitating pessimism of Carrington. But it is fair to say that the Foreign Secretary's stand was neither unreasonable nor illogical. He was himself very much in the Macmillan tradition so far as Africa was concerned, and he did not wish to see Britain associated with any moves that would suggest hostility to the aspirations of black Africa. Neither could he genuinely see a way ahead where so many others had failed.

One other point was being mulled over by the Prime Minister. At her single meeting with Bishop Muzorewa she had formed the lowest possible view of his competence, and reports reached her from other sources by no means unsympathetic in principle to the theory of a Muzorewa government that his black staff were even worse. None of this helped the new government in Salisbury, nor its prospects for survival.

One date loomed up before Lusaka. On 25 July she had to speak to the House of Commons in the final debate before the summer recess; and she would have to speak at length about policy over Rhodesia. In the preceding days drafts arrived from various quarters suggesting all manner of forms of words. On 22 July, according to an aide who had recently discussed the matter at length with her, she was moving towards a new proposal, which would be an amalgam of many others. She would, it seemed, advocate a constitutional conference in London, at which all parties to the dispute would be represented. Any party or faction which failed to show up would, so far as the United Kingdom was concerned, be left out in the cold, but the conference would be followed by a general election supervised by a British governor, and Britain would recognise whatever régime was thus created.

This was less of a high-risk policy than it might seem on the surface. Some of her advisers feared that Ian Smith – and, perhaps, even more significantly, his Army commander General Peter Walls – would turn the proposal down out of hand. However, Mrs Thatcher knew by now that South Africa, though without any great enthusiasm, would support the attendance of Smith and Muzorewa, and would exert pressure to secure it. She was more concerned at the prospect of a Mugabe refusal, for Mugabe had been intransigently insistent that it was Britain's sole remaining function in the affair simply to recognise the Patriotic Front.

In any event, the speech of 25 July went off quietly. Except by Julian Amery it was not widely noted that it represented a significant retreat from her assumed position of willingness to recognise Muzorewa. In Salisbury there was profound gloom. But when, a few days later, I took a copy of the relevant *Hansard* to President Kaunda in Lusaka he executed a little jig of glee around his desk. The stage was set for the Prime Ministers' conference.

Kaunda's willingness to approve of Margaret Thatcher – qualified as it was – was not shared by other Commonwealth leaders. From afar, Mugabe and Nkomo watched in profound unease. Edgar Tekere, the former's observer in Lusaka, made a bitter denunciation of the British Prime Minister. The arrangements for her arrival at Lusaka airport were chaotic, and security men feared that she would be assaulted. Her opening address to the conference, however, if it did not remove all suspicions, completely changed the situation, for in it she condemned the so-called 'internal settlement' as defective because it gave disproportionate power to the whites, and propounded the idea of a constitutional conference in London.

There followed immediately the establishment of a 'contact group' – Britain, Zambia, Tanzania, Nigeria, Jamaica and Australia. Its meetings were curious affairs, and had it not been for the increasing rapport between Mrs Thatcher and President Kaunda they might easily have broken down. (Indeed, on one occasion only the timely intervention of her husband ended a gathering at which she was on the verge of losing her temper.)

Mrs Thatcher's advocacy of a constitutional conference went a long way towards taking the wind out of the sails of her critics. However, she had a sticking point which, refuelling suspicion as it did, and provoking as it did the almost hysterical opposition of Robert Mugabe, bade fair to wreck the proceedings of the contact group.

She was determined that the constitutional conference would, like those which had led to independence for so many British colonies, take place under exclusively British chairmanship. More: the elections which were to follow, she insisted, would take place under the authority of a British governor, to whom Smith and Muzorewa would surrender the authority Smith had seized in 1965. Still more: the election would be policed by British forces and, before they took place, the guerrillas in Rhodesia would assemble at designated points and lay down their arms, though the same strict conditions would not apply to the existing Rhodesian forces under the command of General Walls. There would be no Commonwealth forces, though there could be Commonwealth observers. Most certainly there would be neither military nor political involvement by the United Nations.

This formula was, understandably, hard for most of the black leaders to accept. To Mrs Thatcher's repeated demand that they trust both her and whoever she sent out they replied with a mixture of evasion and hostility. Their reaction, in turn, provoked her to the verge of anger. However, in spite of Carrington's repeated pleas for compromise she would not budge and eventually, with the mollifying aid of Kenneth Kaunda and Malcolm Fraser, she had her way.

I have dwelt at length on these preliminaries to the Lancaster House conference which brought Rhodesia to independence as Zimbabwe in order to draw out and emphasise the crucial strategic rôle of the Prime Minister. Carrington was to conduct the exchanges at Lancaster House with great skill, but it was she who made the vital decisions. 'If my dear Margaret', Kenneth Kaunda said to me over lunch the day after the conference ended, 'had not been so wise, if she had listened to your Foreign Office types' – here he mimicked a glum expression – 'we would have got nowhere and blood would have run all over Southern Africa. My own country might have been ruined.' President Kaunda is fond of metaphors drawn from soccer, and he concluded, 'She was a star centre-forward. So many others were just destroying full-backs.'

The unspoken assumption that underlay the agreement of the contact group was that Britain – probably in some sort of agreement with South Africa – would deliver Muzorewa, Smith and Sithole to the conference table. Nkomo would be delivered by Kaunda, from within whose borders his wing of the Patriotic Front operated, while Mugabe would be persuaded to attend by yet another African leader, Samora Machel of Mozambique, where the second Patriotic Front leader had his bases. Both Zambia and Mozambique, it should be remembered, had suffered terribly from the Rhodesian war, the former country being struck again and again by the Rhodesians, the latter by the South Africans. Both were ready for a formula of negotiation that would – or could – lead to a genuine black majority government. This imposition on them of the necessity of accepting something less than their ideal solution – one of victory – was to appear again during the Lancaster House negotiations.

In everybody's opinion there was no time to be lost. The conference opened in the second week of September, and all the interested parties attended. The opening was the occasion for the passing of responsibility from the Prime Minister to Carrington: he was the conference chairman, the relevant senior minister, and almost as inexperienced in conducting the affairs of such a gathering as she had been in influencing the preliminary colloquy in Lusaka.

However, he was not without advantages. He had a clear – even a rigid – framework of instructions. From the British point of view the conference *must* have a positive conclusion. It should result in a general election under British authority in which all the potential participants – Smith, Muzorewa, Mugabe, Nkomo, Sithole and even outsiders like the minor faction leader James Chikerama, who was not represented at the conference proper – would take part. If unanimity of participation could not be achieved, the next best result would be a general election with some of the participants at the conference taking part. If that second-best solution was unavailable, then Britain would step down from her rôle of responsible power for the future of Rhodesia.

In practice that third outcome was never a likely one, unless there was something amounting to a white *coup d'état*. Muzorewa and Smith were always prepared to accept a fresh election, and British supervision. Though unkindly meant in the way in which it was expressed, the account given by one of Mugabe's aides of an apocryphal conversation between Muzorewa and Carrington was not unfair. In the story Carrington telephoned Muzorewa and began the conversation, 'Abel, will you . . .' Muzorewa interrupted him with, 'Peter, before you go on, yes, of course.'

Given the rigidity of the framework, Carrington had another advantage, perhaps most important in terms of British domestic politics, but not without significance in the wider framework of international relations as well. This was the unqualified support and trust of the Prime Minister. He was not empowered to allow negotiations to take off in any direction that might break the agreement of Lusaka – nor did he want them to – but so far as the tactics of exchanges were concerned he might conduct himself as he pleased, always certain that he could turn to Downing Street for the most resolute, and resonant backing. While she was still in the early months of her prime ministership Mrs Thatcher was already gaining a reputation, abroad as well as at home, among her critics as well as her admirers, as a woman of her word. As Edison Zvobgo – theoretically the media spokesman for the Patriotic Front as a whole, in practice Robert Mugabe's man – said towards the end, 'The voice was his voice, the thought was hers.'

Within the framework, however, there were preferences. As regards the character of the constitution itself, the British government were not prepared to accept white dominance of Rhodesia; but nor were they prepared to accept a formula that did not allow the whites an entrenched parliamentary position, at least for a number of years. As regards the parties to the conference, the British team hoped for the triumph of Nkomo in the elections. Robert Mugabe was, to them, the undesirable outsider.

There were a number of reasons for this view. Nkomo was the longest-serving and the senior figure in the black Rhodesian independence movement. Throughout his career he had shown himself willing to consider compromises with white interests. And, if he had often authorised or encouraged violence, then so had Jomo Kenyatta, the

President of Kenya, and every British government's favourite African leader. True Joshua (one can only express the general friendliness of British attitudes to Nkomo at this time by emphatic reference to the fact that he was almost always referred to in private conversation by his Christian name) had had a great record of dealing with the Russians and the East Germans. But that was put down to his sense of tactics: his known personal friendship with Mr Roland 'Tiny' Rowland, the chief executive of the multinational corporation Lonrho, and the known fact that Lonrho was paying many of his bills in London, encouraged the view that he was 'no red', as one of Mrs Thatcher's office put it.

Muzorewa was discounted, partly because he had evidently compromised himself in black eyes by allying himself with Ian Smith before all the possibilities of war and diplomacy had been exhausted, partly because of serious doubts about his capacity. The other black leaders were of no weight.

Against Mugabe there were several stripes. His rhetoric was consistently, eloquently, even virulently Marxist. He thrust his views into prominence so frequently – in private, or in public, it made no difference – that an assumption of Communism attached itself to him even though, in fairly stark contrast to Joshua Nkomo, he had had no dealings of any moment with the powers of Eastern Europe. He was touchy in the extreme: from the moment of his arrival in London on 7 September he objected to all arrangements, even – or especially – those made for his comfort and security. Conscious of the fact that he was junior to Nkomo in length of service to black independence in Rhodesia (the product of a difference in years, not attitude) he was proud of the intransigence he had so often manifested.

He was also a Shona, as was Muzorewa. Nkomo was the effective king of the minority tribe, the 'Ndebele. It therefore seemed possible to many in London (including the present writer) that in an election the Shona vote would split and that Nkomo could emerge as the victorious leader of a Shona–'Ndebele–white coalition. It was not until Lord Soames went out to Rhodesia as Governor, appraised the situation with an experienced and acute eye, and concluded that Mugabe was the inevitable victor, that scales of hope began to drop from London eyes.

So far as the Lancaster House negotiations were concerned, however, practicality rather than preference was the order of Carrington's day. It mattered less to him *who* should win an election in Rhodesia than that there should be a resolution and that, one way or another, Britain should be quit of responsibility. He wanted – he worked exceptionally hard, and often brilliantly – to achieve a resolution which would involve all parties in an election, but early on he identified Mugabe as the most likely outsider, so much of his time and energy was devoted to pushing Mugabe from point to point.

He was never particularly bothered by gestures from either Smith or Muzorewa. On 27 October he forced Muzorewa, by the threat of British disavowal of the Bishop's government, to accept its dissolution, and the handing over of its authority to a governor. Immediately afterwards General Walls arrived in London and declared his ability to continue the war to a successful conclusion – provided British proposals for an election were accepted, and sanctions lifted. On the other hand Walls made it clear – readily in private, never in public – that he was prepared to accept, would even welcome an election in which all participants to the conflict were engaged.

It has to be said that the Thatcher government was exceptionally fortunate in the matter of timing. South African disenchantment and the fears of Presidents Kaunda and Machel for the stability of their own countries reached climax at the same time. Nkomo and Sithole were, in any event, men predisposed in favour of a diplomatic solution, in line with the general tradition of British withdrawal from colonial responsibilities in Africa. Many in the white business community in Salisbury – numbers of whom I spoke to around this time – were convinced that the siege economy in which they operated could not last much longer. In the words of one of them – himself a South African – 'There's a limit to what you can do with elastic bands and paper clips. Everything here is starting to run down. The fighting's just got to stop.' It is fair to say that the number of whites, who formed the backbone of the business and agricultural communities of Rhodesia, who approached with any degree of relish the prospect of a black government for their country, was tiny. Most took the same view of the future as did a senior member of the Salisbury Stock Exchange who told me, 'I love this country and it's been damn good to me. But I'm having my kids educated in America. Any black government, even if it's one led by Mugabe, will be sensible enough to let me see my time out here. But there's no long-term future for the white man.' And, indeed, as the war intensified more and more white Rhodesians, especially those who were themselves immigrants from Britain, were taking the road south – to the Republic of South Africa – or, as the men and women of harder will put it, 'the traitor's road'.

Of all the participants in the prolonged conflict, and of all those assembled in London, only Robert Mugabe seemed to have much stomach for a prolongation of battle. Ian Smith, it is true, the very symbol of white intransigence over the years, returned home in the middle of the conference. But this was not, as the Foreign Office for a time feared, indicative of a determination to organise resistance in the last ditch. Smith, a man of very considerable parts, and of some real vision – quite apart from his possession of remarkable tactical political skill – realised, quite simply, that the end of his adventure was approaching, and he wanted as little part as possible in the devising of a new constitution for his country. Once it was clear to him that whatever formula emerged at Lancaster House it would provide for reserved parliamentary seats for the whites and give them, moreover some (at least temporary) means of resisting further constitutional change such as would serve Mugabe's declared ambition of creating a one party state in the new Zimbabwe, he felt that his rôle was finished.

Even Mugabe had a shock in store. Ideologically – as well as personally – ascetic to the point of primness he has all the self-belief, and powers of endurance, of a fanatic. The contrast, during the weeks in London, between his austere conduct and the sybaritic tastes of many of his entourage was marked. The ordered structure of his rhetoric, whether in public or around the conference table, was in singular opposition to that of his friends and rivals alike, and perhaps it was in the matter of conduct that he differed most sharply from Joshua Nkomo, enormous, agreeable and as rambling in speech as he was in gait. Mugabe often spoke with passion, and Mugabe often lost his temper, or appeared to do so: but about everything he did there was a kind of icy control. That control covered an undoubted willingness to take matters to the limit. He knew – it could not have been made more obvious – that the British looked to Nkomo for the future. This awareness on his part intensified the natural paranoia of a man who had been so long in prison and so long in the bush. When he became convinced, therefore, that Carrington was seeking to manoeuvre the conference against him he departed without warning for

Mozambique, to assure himself of Machel's continued support. He was told, with many expressions of regret, that it would not be forthcoming, and that the time had come when Samora Machel had to take thought for his own nation. Kenneth Kaunda took the trouble to travel to London himself, so that the leaders of the Patriotic Front would be in no doubt that they had to settle for whatever was now available. Of African leaders the most important to advise continued intransigence on the part of the PF was Julius Nyerere, President of Tanzania, who had not himself attended the Lusaka conference and could not, therefore, appreciate the significance of the rapport that had been achieved in the capital of Zambia between that country's President and the British Prime Minister. The alliance, personal as well as political, between Margaret Thatcher and Kenneth Kaunda, was crucial to the outcome of the Rhodesian rebellion.

The history of politics abounds in irony. Kaunda had for years put his own country at risk to secure the emergence of a black-ruled Zimbabwe. Margaret Thatcher, within weeks of becoming Prime Minister, became convinced that it was in the best interests of the United Kingdom to accede to Kaunda's line. Both President and Prime Minister, however, hoped against hope that the black who ruled would be Joshua Nkomo who was, after all, Zambia's client. The Foreign Office persisted almost to the end in the belief that Nkomo would emerge triumphant from an electoral confrontation, and therefore govern Zimbabwe in alliance with Bishop Muzorewa. Kaunda's end was achieved in that Zimbabwe passed to black rule; but he was frustrated in that the black ruler was hostile to him, and to Zambia. Much the same applied, *pari passu*, to Margaret Thatcher. For the Foreign Secretary, and for his Office, there was simply great relief that the debilitating years of conflict with Ian Smith and his supporters was over.

Next to the Falklands war the creation of an independent and internationally recognised Zimbabwe was the most dramatic event of Margaret Thatcher's first term as Prime Minister. It is an event, moreover, that still gives rise to intense controversy, and that controversy centres on the debate not only about whether what was done was right, but about who was responsible for doing it. That debate, finally, is immensely significant in the business of unveiling the whole nature of British attitudes to international relations in recent years.

Broadly speaking there are two schools of thought. Whatever criticism they will accept of Carrington his supporters none the less see the creation of Zimbabwe as a crowning achievement. The most enthusiastic supporters of the Prime Minister, on the other hand, tending to be people who heartily dislike what has happened in Zimbabwe since independence, are only too happy to attribute the major responsibility for events to Carrington. His admirers and his detractors are thus at one.

I have already made it clear that, in my judgement – as in that of Mr Stephenson[3] – the major burden of responsibility for the turn taken in British policy on central Africa between 1979 and 1980 rests with Margaret Thatcher. I happen to believe, further, that her decision to ally herself with Kenneth Kaunda and so to organise matters that there would emerge in Rhodesia a black government acceptable to the international community was a correct one: the cost to Britain of any alternative procedure was too high to be acceptable. The whole sequence of events, however, offers much instruction in different approaches to international relations and diplomacy.

The attitude of the new Foreign Secretary in May 1979 was essentially a pessimistic one, and his pessimism was fully shared by his officials. The attitude of the new Prime Minister, on the other hand, was essentially optimistic. It was a contrast between world-weariness and hopefulness. The Foreign Office saw in Rhodesia a difficulty that had resisted the best efforts of successive governments. Even in the Conservative Party, the ranks of which were filled by those who venerated his diplomatic expertise, there were many who could not believe that their new heroine could succeed where Lord Home had failed. In No 10 Downing Street under the new dispensation, however, problems existed only to be cracked: the breeziness of the attitude there was in marked contrast to that across the road in the Scott building.

From whichever angle one approached it, however, the Rhodesian problem offered a series of choices, a series, indeed, of predictable ends. It was open to the new British government to recognise the government headed by Bishop Muzorewa, and to live with the consequences in terms of international and Commonwealth alienation. It

3. Hugh Stephenson, *Mrs Thatcher's First Year* (London, 1980), p. 82ff.

is right to add, here, that any such action was certain to be viewed with extreme displeasure in Buckingham Palace. Her Majesty the Queen did, indeed, display emphatic disapproval of a suggestion that she should not, on grounds of security, preside over the Lusaka conference. 'The Queen', explained one of her staff, 'is Head of the Commonwealth. It is in that capacity that she will go to Lusaka. She is not open to advice from her British government on the matter.' It was also open to Britain simply to wash her hands of the problem and resign all conduct of the matter to the United Nations: in the Labour Party there were, indeed, some advocates of such a course of action. Finally, it was open to Mrs Thatcher and her Cabinet to do what she did, and through a constitutional conference to bring about the death of the old Rhodesia and the birth of the new Zimbabwe. Whatever policy was adopted, however, there was a foreseeable end to the whole business.

The resolution of this Gordian knot was not, however, available in other areas of British foreign policy. The nation's relations with other member states of the European Economic Community, her place in the Atlantic Alliance, and her continuing responsibility for various other territories around the world, most notably the Falkland Islands, Belize and Hong Kong, made up a seamless web of continuing diplomacy. In the management of these affairs the respective attitudes of Prime Minister and Foreign Office were in as sharp a contrast as they were over Rhodesia.

I have already made mention of the debilitating effect of these different attitudes in so far as the EEC was concerned.[4] Again the difference was between a politician who believed that effort could produce results, and one who feared that action would damage an existing and desirable structure. It was an article of faith in the Foreign Office that securing the full acceptance of Britain by her continental European partners was the principal – sometimes it seemed the only – end of foreign policy. Diplomats were acutely aware of the fact that, on their reading of history, the United Kingdom had lost out badly by standing aloof for so many years from the nascent EEC.[5] Time was,

4. Above, p. 14.
5. For an elegant recent statement of this view see Brendan Donnelly, *European Document: a reply to Patrick Cosgrave*, in *The American Spectator*, April 1985.

they thought, required to repair the consequences of past omissions. Britain had still a good part of her passage to work in Europe, and it followed, therefore, that her principal activity should be of conciliation, not conflict. Between 1979 and 1982 Carrington, in the assessment of one of his staff, spent more than eighty per cent of his time on matters directly or indirectly concerned with European policy. His assiduity in this area of policy was often remarked upon, and was held to be in sharp contrast to the cavalier behaviour of his Prime Minister. It was felt, indeed, that he saw himself as bound by industry to repair the damage done by prime ministerial rhetoric and conduct.

In this period, therefore, relations with the United States suffered, particularly after the election of Ronald Reagan in 1980. The Prime Minister and the President felt an instant affinity with each other: like her he promised to be radical in his conduct of domestic policy, and there were a great many ready points of contact between her and his intellectual spear-carriers. Indeed, the years of her party leadership saw a remarkable growth in relations between the apostles of the new Conservatism in Britain and the new Republicanism in the United States, a growth which was symbolised by the influence on her thinking about East–West relations by Dr Robert Conquest, the English historian of modern Russia who now lives in America, and the recall from the International Monetary Fund of Professor Alan Walters to act as her personal economic adviser. No similar nexus of personal relations exists between British Tories close to the Prime Minister and political society in any of the major continental countries. In the European Assembly, for example, British Conservatives enjoy a formal relationship only with their Danish opposite numbers: although there are, naturally, a great number of points of affinity on general policy there are no institutional ties with the West German and Italian Christian Democrats or the French Gaullists.

It was evident, moreover, from 1975 onwards that questions of taste and natural sympathy were to be of consequence in the political equation. To put the matter simply, and even crudely, Margaret Thatcher likes Americans and American society and is, by and large, indifferent to Europeans and European society. 'Her eyes gleam', said one of her private staff, 'when a trip to the States is in the offing. In Europe she just does her duty.' When her then Political Secretary, Richard Ryder (now a Conservative backbencher) took to describing the more enthusiastic proponents of British membership of the EEC as 'Eurofreaks' she gave his formulation benign approval.

All of this created dismay at the Foreign Office. It was, of course, true that the Office came only gradually to the acceptance of an essentially European rôle for Britain: the new cause once embraced, however, enthusiasm for it knew no bounds. The more readily Atlantic attitude of the Prime Minister was something to be deplored and, if possible, undone. To the Office the ideal order of priorities was that obtaining when Edward Heath was Prime Minister: he chose to be deliberately dismissive of the Anglo-American relationship in order the better to authenticate his European credentials. In all essentials on this admittedly difficult and troubling question Carrington was a Heath man.

It is a characteristic of his on which I have already remarked that he invariably tries to conform to the perceived requirements of his job: these requirements having been defined, there is no need for further speculation or philosophising, or for trying to impose his character or his will on the institution of which he is a part. It is interesting, by way of illustration, to note how the American view of him has changed since he became, in 1984, Secretary-General of NATO. In that Alliance, of course, the United States is the dominant partner. Aware of the fact that his years as Foreign Secretary had earned him the suspicion, and in some cases the downright dislike of senior politicians in the Reagan administration, a number of whom had opposed his NATO appointment,[6] Carrington immediately set himself to repair his fences. 'I'm honestly quite amazed', an American diplomat of great experience observed to me, 'how pro-us the guy has suddenly become.' While at the Foreign Office, however, Carrington saw it as his duty to make up to the European powers for his Prime Minister's seemingly extravagant liking for her American opposite number.

His very method of working, further, enhanced the intimacy he enjoyed with his Foreign Office officials. His favourite annotation on memoranda, he told Terry Coleman in the *Guardian* on 27 March 1982, was 'Speak'. He added, of paperwork submitted to him

I'd rather see the guy who wrote it and talk to him. Much

6. Below, p. 164.

easier, you know, seeing people – certainly for me – than the written word because the written word is very, very, particularly here, very carefully drafted. These guys are all absolute wizards with the written word.

It is understandable that a minister should pay a compliment to his officials. It is, indeed, civilised of him to do so. But there is, in Carrington's words to Coleman, an expression of awe that I find unbecoming.

It is, of course, true that indecisiveness in Britain about relations with the United States as opposed to those with continental Europe was less than novel in 1979. In his fine study of British foreign policy since 1916[7] F. S. Northedge analysed, with a perspicuity which no other student has demonstrated, the inability of the United Kingdom indefinitely to sustain what Anthony Eden described as a policy with three legs, one being Europe, one the United States and one the Commonwealth. Once, under Harold Macmillan – though more definitely when Edward Heath was Prime Minister – the decision was taken to seek membership of the EEC, with all that involved in the way of agreement to the Common Agricultural Policy, the Commonwealth leg of the tripod was knocked away. The Commonwealth did not, of course, die: the House of Windsor, not to mention shared language and heritage, sustained it. But from the date of the signature of the Treaty of Brussels in 1972 the message was clear – that the United Kingdom now set greater store by her European connections than she did by her ancient relations with the relics of her Empire now grouped together as the Commonwealth of Nations. Evidence of the importance of this new attachment was available in the price paid by the primary food-producing countries of the Commonwealth in their restricted access to the British market: transitional arrangements, certainly, were made, and arguments about the CAP continues. But the fact of the matter remained that from now on it was determined that Britain would deal with the Commonwealth for all practical purposes as a member of a European grouping.

In 1979 there remained, however, the United States. It has become increasingly clear since the return to office of the Conservative Party in that year that there is a serious difference of economic interest on a

7. *The Uncertain Giant* (London, 1967).

number of matters between Western Europe, considered as a whole, and the United States.[8] At the same time the combination of recession at home and the unfavourable budgetary arrangements made with the EEC by the Heath government meant that the Thatcher government was constantly disruptive of the Community and continually insistent on making money out of, rather than paying money into it. 'I cannot', the Prime Minister told an EEC summit at Strasbourg in 1979, 'play Sister Bountiful to the Community. . .'

Her attitude was, to her Foreign Secretary and his department, both offensive and alarming. It was offensive, too, to the continental powers: they had, after all, been listening to British pleas for membership of their group since 1961, in which year Harold Macmillan had made the first bid.[9] It was difficult for them to sympathise with a British government that, to their mind, seemed determined to break the rules of association and was, at the same time so decisively in favour of the United States. It fell to Carrington, therefore, to attempt to explain, in Brussels and other capitals, that Margaret Thatcher was not the whole of the British Government.

I have already mentioned how destructive of, and how weakening to national policy was this difference of attitude between a department of government and the head of that government.[10] No sense of constitutional propriety, however, inhibited either the Foreign Secretary or his officials from implying to their European colleagues that their attitude would be more *communautaire* if only Mrs Thatcher would allow it. The country lost badly by this division, for there was neither a benefit to be gained from Foreign Office complaisance, nor from Mrs Thatcher's intransigence. The rule must, therefore, be restated: it is improper for a department of state to make policy, or to be allowed to seem to be making policy, apart from a Cabinet and Prime Minister.

There was more to this, however, than a difference over policy. There was a difference of method which, in Carrington's case, involved the exaltation of technique over aim.

8. Patrick Cosgrave, *America versus Europe*, in *Policy Review* (Washington, Summer 1982).
9. Harold Macmillan, *Britain, the Commonwealth and Europe* (London, Conservative Political Centre, 1961).
10. Above, p. 124.

In September 1981, according to Lord Franks,[11] Carrington wrote, à propos of the endless frustration of diplomatic dealing with Argentina, that there was 'little we can do beyond trying to keep some sort of negotiation going'. He thus displayed, according to the *Daily Telegraph* on 19 January 1983, 'a mystical belief in negotiation as something which can go on when there is nothing to be bargained for and therefore nothing to be discussed'. We are, therefore, back with the heart of the argument of this book: that the Foreign Office, with the enthusiastic connivance of its chief, sedulously pursued, between 1979 and 1982, a policy at odds with the declared policy of the government of the day and, moreover, judged its own activity of diplomacy to be, by itself, a good deal greater than any other in international relations.

The 'impression of their independence' to which Northedge refers in *The Foreign Policies of the Powers*[12] when discussing the activities of nations in the international arena may be based on illusion. It is, none the less, political fact, and in foreign policy the business of a government is to maximise its freedom of action. It is not necessary to be a super-power, nor even a great power, to enjoy a satisfactory degree of freedom of action. Indeed, freedom of action is enjoined on some powers simply by virtue of their geopolitical position. Israel, for example, simply because of her isolation in her area of the world, has little choice but to insist, through her local military power, on the most emphatic freedom of action when she considers her interests to be threatened. In a like – but non-military – manner Switzerland has eschewed membership of all the main international institutions – including the United Nations – simply because the ultimate priority of successive Swiss governments has been to preserve the independence of their country. This tough-minded attitude has not, of course, prevented Switzerland from profiting from playing hostess to innumerable international bodies.

The fundamental position of the Foreign Office for a generation, and of Peter Carrington from 1979 to 1982, has been that Britain cannot, and in any event should not, act alone. Now, it is true that nations can very rarely act alone. Israel, to return to the example just

11. Falkland Islands Review.
12. Above, p. 139.

mentioned, depends on the United States for the sinews of her military machine. During the war for the Falklands Britain depended to some considerable extent on the goodwill of the United States and the EEC powers to achieve her aim of regaining sovereignty over the islands. The difference is between an attitude of mind that stresses above all the desirability of alliance, and one which seeks, above all, to increase the international leverage enjoyed by any particular power. Peter Carrington embodies the first attitude, Margaret Thatcher the second. The difference, put very simply, is between a non-nationalist and a nationalist outlook on international life. Indeed, what makes him historically interesting is the fact that he was both exceptionally eloquent and exceptionally persuasive as the head of a department whose collective view of the world he shared at a time when the head of the government was, in both style and policy, seeking to lead the nation in a different direction from that favoured by the department. Between 1956 and 1979, for all that there were frequent quarrels between the Foreign Office and the government of the day, there was never such sustained mutual incomprehension and hostility between the denizens of the FO and the tenant of No 10 Downing Street. That such incomprehension and hostility existed was plain to Carrington. He deplored it, but he felt he could do little about it. He had no desire to change the policy of the Office; and he had no belief that he could change the policy of the Prime Minister.

How much damage was done to Britain's interests during those years cannot yet be assessed. It could be argued, as I do, that Anglo–European relations were seriously damaged over the whole of Mrs Thatcher's first term by the simple inability of the United Kingdom's continental partners to understand which signals from London they were to believe. It is certainly the case that the all-too-evident antipathy between the Foreign Office and the American State Department set Anglo-American relations back seriously at a time when the good personal relations between President and Prime Minister might have been expected markedly to further them. The Falklands war might have been avoided, and negotiations with the People's Republic of China over Hong Kong more speedily concluded – and without the acrimony which marked their early stages – if British diplomats had set themselves in as dedicated a fashion to the pursuit of the government's objectives as they did to the pursuit of their own.

In 1985, and at the conclusion of her controversial Far Eastern tour, it is surely unquestionable that, to most of the outside world, Margaret Thatcher *is* Britain. It is not necessary to agree with either her objectives or her priorities to see the simple truth of that statement. Nor is it necessary, when accepting that truth, to exaggerate her influence in response to the dramatic rhetoric in which she clothes her thoughts. What is, however, to be lamented is the fact that a Prime Minister of such exceptional force of personality has so rarely enjoyed the unstinted backing of what is, next to the Treasury, the most powerful governmental department in the United Kingdom.

8. THE AFTERMATH

These realities – the recognition at last by the United States of her inescapable position as a world Power, after an almost uninterrupted existence in isolation, and the re-emergence at last of Russia in her rightful place as another world power after twenty-five years of chaos and recovery from revolution – are important. But they are not the only product of years of evolution from one world framework to another, not the only factors that have made the world balance of power more stable since 1946 than it had been at any time in the previous fifty years, and that will keep it so for some long time. It may be said, indeed, that in some respects they have been given too much prominence. The suddenness with which the new equilibrium seemed to emerge has been one reason why men have had difficulty in recognising it. Another has been their misunderstanding of the extent and the nature of Russian and American strength in the post-war years.

F. H. Hinsley, *Power and the pursuit of Peace*
(Cambridge, 1967), p. 353.

The opening of the Falklands war seemed, for a time, to mark the end of Carrington's political career. He was, to be sure, in demand as a public speaker, on such platforms as that provided by the Royal Institute of International Affairs. His virtually immediate assumption of the chairmanship of the General Electric Company seemed to indicate a willing option for private over public life, even if his resolute refusal to entertain any of the many invitiations he received to pen a volume of memoirs suggested that he had not wholly given up hope of a return to the political stage.

On 14 June 1982, however, the Argentinian forces surrendered at Port Stanley. The Prime Minister then asked Lord Franks – who was to be assisted by Lord Barber (a former Conservative Chancellor of the Exchequer), Lord Lever (once a Labour minister), Lord Watkinson (a whilom Tory Defence minister), Merlyn Rees (Home Secretary in the Callaghan government) and Sir Patrick Nairne (a civil servant) – to examine the origins of the war. In January of the following year Lord

Franks reported. To the great surprise of nobody Franks concluded 'that we would not be justified in attaching any criticism or blame to the present government for the Argentine Junta's decision to commit its act of unprovoked aggression in the invasion of the Falkland Islands on 2 April 1982'.[1] In spite of the derision with which this bland judgement was greeted in many quarters it had the effect of lifting officially the cloud that had hung over Carrington. The question of a return to political office began to be discussed.

In June 1983 Mrs Thatcher appealed to the country for a renewal of her mandate. She was rewarded in spectacular fashion. Fifty-eight additions were made to the strength of the Conservative Party in the House of Commons. The party enjoyed a lead of 188 seats over Labour and of 144 over the combined opposition parties. The Prime Minister was virtually unchallengeable. In private she expressed, further, her desire to make some recompense to Carrington for his precipitate departure from office.

There were, however, certain problems. Sir Geoffrey Howe was anxious to quit the Treasury, where he had spent an embattled four years. His heart was set on the Foreign Office and she wished suitably to reward this most committed of her supporters. Carrington, in any event, could hardly be given his old job back: it would be too emphatic an endorsement of his past and would be greeted with outrage in important sections of the Conservative Party. No domestic Cabinet office, given the dispositions she intended to make, was available or, probably, acceptable to him. The only remaining choice open to her was an international post of sufficient distinction.

It happened that Dr Joseph Luns, formerly Dutch Foreign Minister and for fourteen years Secretary-General of the North Atlantic Treaty Organisation, now intimated a desire to retire. Under the prevailing, though informal system of management that has grown up since the signing of the treaty establishing NATO in 1948 the major military command has been invariably held by an American officer and the major political office by a European. It has always, moreover, gone to a citizen of one of the minor European powers; the argument here was that the post of Secretary-General, being honorific rather than power-ful, it could safely be awarded to one of the smaller countries without

1. Falkland Islands Review.

any effect on the real balance of power within the organisation. It could, however, be a useful symbol of the seriousness with which the bigger powers regarded their less mighty confrères. In 1983, however, nobody from Holland, Belgium, Luxembourg, Portugal or Norway put himself forward. The Italians had no candidate, nor did the Germans. No Greek or Turkish candidate was suggested and, indeed, the rivalry between the two powers was such as to preclude a Secretary-General of either nationality. Towards the end of 1983 it became apparent that Carrington was, if not ideal, the only candidate of stature available.

Two questions remained. Did he want the job? Would the Americans accept him? Some of his friends were against the whole idea. 'Can you imagine it?' one of them said to me in disgusted tones, 'Peter in a position of no power and having to sit down again and again with a lot of squabbling Greeks and suchlike?' The suspicion with which the Americans regarded him was fast becoming legendary, and was enshrined in the off-the-cuff remark said to have been made by President Reagan's first Secretary of State, Alexander Haig, that he was 'a duplicitous bastard'.

The answer to the first question was positive. Carrington did want the job, in part at least because it would represent a rehabilitation. And the Americans, in answer to the second question, would accept him because there was nobody else and because Margaret Thatcher very much wanted him. American doubt dissolved rapidly in the face of the Prime Minister's firm argument that it was for the European powers to decide on the Secretary-Generalship. Carrington, moreover, as has already been mentioned, took great pains to make himself agreeable to the major NATO partner. On 25 June 1984 he took up his new post. If he had enjoyed a great deal less power and prestige than he had had between 1979 and 1982 he was none the less again a fully-fledged senior figure in international politics. He took office on a wave of goodwill.

His immediate tone was conciliatory. 'I shall aim', he said[2]

> during my tenure to follow my predecessors: to stimulate, to harmonise and to channel the contributions of all member

2. *NATO Review* (June, 1984).

countries to the good of the Alliance. I shall do everything I can to make sure that its story continues to be one of success.

Whatever doubts there were about him were subsumed in his charm and his intentions. Dr Luns, who was widely believed to have serious reservations about his successor, made a point of giving him a warm welcome. The Falklands chapter was thus closed, and a new one opened.

The thirty-fifth year of NATO's life was the occasion for a great deal of introspection.[3] To this feeling Carrington paid obeisance in his first official message as Secretary-General. 'It has for many years', he wrote,

> been a commonplace to say that NATO is in a state of crisis ... It may in some measure be NATO's success which prompt some in all our countries to ask why, after 40 years of peace, it should be necessary to continue this elaborate and expensive organisation. Experience and a knowledge of history provide the answer: the way to avoid war is to make it known, clearly and without doubt, that we have the means to defend ourselves and the resolution to do so. In the face of the enormous military potential of the Soviet Union, and its unrelenting defence expenditure, it would be an unbelievable folly for the countries of the Alliance to assume that their joint efforts are no longer necessary.

One passage in this message – though it also contained his assurance of continuity – gave a hint of departure from the legacy of Luns. In the course of listing the tasks ahead of the Alliance, Carrington gave, as second in importance only to the maintenance of the credibility of the Western deterrent, the necessity of pursuing disarmament between East and West:

> ... NATO is a political organisation as well as a military one, [therefore] we must continue to seek – as we have done in the past – to reduce the causes of tension between East and

3. Godson, *op. cit.*, and *Cosgrave and Richey, op. cit.*

West, and to reach agreements on arms control and disarmament which are reliable and fair.

These may sound like very unexceptionable aims. But the vital point to
understand is that previous Secretaries-General considered their rôles
to be in the ironing out of differences within NATO, not in making
Alliance policy towards the opposing Warsaw Pact. 'The trouble with
Carrington', grumbled one American critic, 'is that he thinks he's still
a Foreign Minister, not an international civil servant. Only this time he
thinks he's Foreign Minister of NATO, not just of the UK.' The
commitment to negotiate as an ideal of policy, even as a policy, which
is a principle of Foreign Office activity to which I have repeatedly
drawn attention throughout this book, has evidently remained with
Carrington in his new post. It is too early to say whether the ineluctable facts of international power will ensure that he is confined within
very strict limits, or whether he will manage to break out into the
making of policy, perhaps alongside, but perhaps in opposition to, the
collective judgement of the NATO Council, the senior political body
of the Alliance.

A comparison between the Secretary-General of NATO and the
President of the EEC Commission is interesting to make. The Treaty of
Rome, which set up the EEC, expresses an internationalist political
aspiration. Successive Presidents have, therefore, with perfect propriety, insisted on their right to be present at summit meetings as
representatives of – as, indeed, heads of – an organisation which, if
only putatively, has an identity of its own, separate from the individual
identities of the member nations. Because he entertained such pretensions Professor Walter Hallstein, the West German EEC Commission
President, was driven from office by General de Gaulle.[4] The preten-
sion is not without justification, however, for the simple reason that
the object of the EEC is to achieve the creation of a supra-national
identity, an identity which, in the fullness of time, is intended to extend
into all the fields of its members' national life. The NATO powers, on
the other hand, have come together for only one specific and limited
purpose – that of defence against the might of the USSR and its
satellites. Greece, Spain and Portugal could not become members of

4. John Newhouse, *Collision at Brussels* (London, 1966).

the EEC as long as they were under dictatorial sway, for it is an essential proposition of the Community that any nation joining should be a democracy. There was no objection, however, to Portugal, Greece or Turkey being member-states of NATO even while under the sway of, respectively, Mr Salazar, Colonel Papadopoulos, and General Gursel because the only objective of NATO was a military one. It is true, of course, that the NATO charter enshrines certain democratic aspirations, but its fundamental tenet is that democratic and authoritarian states can happily join in alliance against a totalitarian rival. Such a dispensation gives a Secretary-General, at least in theory, very little scope for the development of an independent rôle.

The effectiveness – which, because of the nature of the job, must be limited – of the Secretary-General depends on keeping an absolutely equal balance between the twin poles of the Alliance, the American and the European. Quite apart from all his early and personal activity in assuaging American doubts about his appointment, Carrington went out of his way, in his June 1984 message, to state his view of the proper relationship between the senior partner of the Alliance and her European allies. He insisted that each of the European member states

> have some responsibility for maintaining in good repair the many links between the United States and Europe. The Atlantic gap cannot be wished away, and understandable differences of perception will persist. But they must not be allowed to obscure the interests or undermine the objectives which we have in common.

Again, the sentiment expressed is unexceptionable. The difficulty is that, at this stage of his career, almost everything he says comes tainted with ambiguity. 'What does he mean', asked one American puzzling over the passage just quoted. 'What's the Atlantic gap supposed to be? Does he think we're Argies?'

The point is a highly pertinent one. At no stage, in so far as we can now see, did Carrington, as Foreign Secretary, give the Argentinian government any direct indication that either he or his department favoured their claims to sovereignty over the Falkland Islands to the extent that he (or they) would be willing to renege on the undertakings given by successive British governments to the islanders. What to them seemed significant was his manner: the manner, if not the words, seemed to indicate indifference. Their sense of that indifference may have emboldened them to behave as they did on 2 April 1982.

Many American politicians – and there are indications that General Bernard Rogers, the Supreme Allied Commander, Europe shares their apprehension – feel that the literal meaning of Carrington's words do not convey his full intention. And they fear, further, that it is his intention less to act as the most visible political spokesman of the Alliance than to act the part of a European spokesman within it, to act, in other words, just as he did when he was Foreign Secretary, and played his part in devising, among other initiatives, the EEC Venice Declaration on the Middle East.

His pronouncements on the American Strategic Defence Initiative (vulgarly called the Star Wars proposal) will be of the greatest interest in the coming years. The SDI is so far from completion that its place in the future of international relations must remain open to question. European fears about its development are, however, susceptible of simple explanation. The intention is to examine the feasibility of creating an anti-ballistic missile system so efficient that it can ensure the destruction of any hostile nuclear weapons fired in anger. Many European politicians doubt the desirability, let alone the feasibility, of such a proposal. They fear that, if the United States, through the building of some SDI system, can make herself secure against aggression then her interest in defending Europe will correspondingly decline.

The American reply is, first, that any SDI screen will cover Western Europe as well and, second, that the greater the security provided for the domestic territory of the United States the greater will be American willingness to reply with nuclear weapons to any Warsaw Pact intrusion in Western Europe. The American element in the Western deterrent has always consisted in both the presence of American troops – 600,000 in all – on European soil and the declared will of United States governments if necessary to respond to any aggression in Europe with nuclear weapons. Those in Europe who have doubted the quality of the American commitment have wondered whether any American President would order a nuclear response to an attack on Berlin if such a response put at risk the lives of the inhabitants of Chicago or New York. If in the future, say the Americans, their country could render herself secure from any trans-continental nuclear attack would she not be all the more willing to engage in war on behalf of a Western European outpost? We already know, however, that Mrs Thatcher and Carrington's successor, Sir Geoffrey Howe – to name only two major European politicians – do not see things quite that way.[5]

Their fear is that the creation of any impregnable defence system for the United States will lead, by inevitable steps, to the withdrawal – for budgetary reasons – of American divisions now on the ground in Britain and continental Europe. Such a process of withdrawal would, undoubtedly, be accompanied by the fairest of promises about the continuing undertaking of the major English-speaking power to defend her allies in Europe. However, given the burgeoning interests of the United States in the Pacific, it is not difficult to imagine a future tenant of the White House who might decide, perhaps under economic pressure, to abandon defence of Western Europe in order the better to serve his country's interests on the other side of the world.

For the moment, however, Europe is the only spot on the globe where American and Russian troops face one another. In the years before the First World War French generals concluded[6] that a serious commitment on the part of the United Kingdom to place even a single soldier on the continent to act in defence of either France or Belgium would be sufficient evidence of her determination to resist encroachment in the west by Germany. French confidence was well-founded. In the last quarter of the twentieth century the similar presence of American troops summarises a similar assurance. No alternative and technological guarantee has the same weight – or moral value – as bodies in place.

It follows from this that the fundamental interest of all the Western European powers is the continued presence of American troops on their continent. To argue with the United States about whether the SDI scheme is desirable or possible is to put at risk the human commitment of American youth to European freedom. If a government in Washington, of whatever colour, concludes that the SDI is an available option it will take it up. If the European attitude is hostile – or even critical –

---

5. Kristol, op. cit.
6. George Monger, The End of Isolation: British foreign policy 1900–1907 (London, 1963).

some of the SDI bill may well be met by the withdrawal of American conventional cover in Western Europe.[7]

It is imaginable, if unlikely, that the Western European powers, and particularly those possessed of a nuclear capacity – that means Britain and France – could put together sufficient communal resources to resist any Soviet thrust against their territory. The basic guarantee of the continuance of the *status quo* in Europe, however, is the presence of American troops on the ground. Although he has been most careful, so far at any rate, to accede to the idea that the SDI should be investigated, and that the question of deployment should be considered later, Carrington, on all the evidence so far available, seems to be putting himself into the position of a European critic of American ideas on strategy. It could easily be fatal to the Western Alliance if its senior civilian officer failed to understand that his foremost duty was to the Alliance as a whole rather than to his own geographical area in particular. When Alexander Haig, for example, was Supreme Allied Commander, Europe, he, although an American officer, made no bones about criticising the defence preparedness of his country. General Bernard Rogers had been likewise forthright. Both men have been understood, even by those who disagreed with them, to be seeking to state the military interest of the Alliance as a whole. No such understanding appears to attend Carrington.

It would be odd if it did. For all the plausibility of his manner, and the devotion which he is capable of exciting, his record in office is less than impressive.

A resumé of his political career makes depressing reading. As Parliamentary Under Secretary of State for Agriculture he could be considered, with reason, at least faulty in his judgement. As First Lord of the Admiralty he was less than sensitive to warnings of espionage within his department: he was, further, somewhat less than attentive to Lord Radcliffe's advice carefully to examine the security system of that department. As Leader of the House of Lords he misjudged the force of the Labour government's feeling on Rhodesia, and thus destroyed the prospect for a reform of the House of Lords on which, as agreed between the major parties, he had set his heart. As Chairman of the Conservative Party he argued, with impeccable logic but an almost

7. Alun Chalfont, *SDI: the case for the defence* (London, 1985).

total lack of political sensitivity, for an early general election which proved to have a disastrous result. As Foreign Secretary and, thus, the minister responsible for bringing some end to the Rhodesian rebellion he wavered between depression for the prospect of any agreeable result, and optimism that the preferred candidate of the British government would win. As Foreign Secretary, again, he misread Argentinian intentions in the South Atlantic, allowed his attention and energy to be diverted from what was his – and his government's – most immediate and pressing problem and, in his own regretful words, 'got it wrong'.

The question, therefore, is how he will fare in what is virtually certain to be his last major post?

The Secretary-General of NATO requires, even apart from an ability to keep all the member states of the Alliance in an agreed balance, a capacity intellectually to understand the threat which the North Atlantic Treaty Organisation was designed, from its origins, to counter. More was asked from Dr Joseph Luns, and more is asked from Lord Carrington, than an ability sensitively to respond to the likes and dislikes, the pride and the hurt, of nations who came together in fear and who live together, and work together, because, at bottom, they believe that the security of each individual country depends on the security of them all.

But does Carrington understand intellectually, let alone emotionally, the instincts of the Alliance of which he is now the main spokesman? He has been, more than once, robust in his rebukes of Soviet pretensions. 'The West itself', he told the House of Lords on 24 January 1980, 'needs to find ways to make the Russians understand that they cannot breach the rules of international behaviour with impunity . . .' But this formulation stood in sad contrast to an earlier one. 'When the chips are down', he told the Royal Institute of International Affairs on 22 February 1980, 'we are all firmly on the side of the only super-power we have.' It is not with such a tone that the people of a democratic power like the United States can be persuaded to continue the commitment of their treasure, and to promise, if necessary, the commitment of their blood to the defence of allies across an ocean.

The most characteristic response of Carrington to a political challenge is a shrug, perhaps enlivened by a quip. His favourite tone is that of irony: he employs both the word and the tone with regularity. Thus, when he was justifiably angry with African and international suspicion of British intentions in Rhodesia in 1980, he observed (to the House of Lords on 6 February 1980) in caustic tone, 'It is ironic that the British Government, which is trying in the most difficult circumstances to hold free and fair elections in Rhodesia should be lectured ... by countries which would not know a free and fair election if they saw it.' The trouble about him is that such moments of energy are moments, and no more. When in a temper he can be decisive; but the temper rarely lasts.

It is possible to see flashes of intellectual energy in Carrington's speeches over the years. Whatever he has managed, however, he has never been able to sustain the kind of bleak and detailed critique of reality such as Lord Home offered to the House of Lords on 23 April 1985. In 1971 Home, then Foreign Secretary, expelled 105 Soviet diplomats from London stating, brutally, that it was his conviction that they were spies. In his eighty-first year he addressed himself again to relations between the Russian empire and the Western world in the hard tones evident in the quotation from him with which I began this book. 'In the past', said Lord Home,

> we have been dealing with the prototype of a Communist state, the ideology of which permeated its foreign policy, which aimed at the promotion of Communism outside Russia's borders, and was ready, on occasion, to use force at first or second hand to achieve a political end.
>
> My Lords, some argue that the idealism in the original Communist conception was corrupted by Stalin in his crude ambition for power and empire. There may be an element of truth in that diagnosis. However, my Lords, some years ago I asked Mr Chou en-Lai to explain to me the working of the Russian Communist mind in relation to Russia's foreign policy and negotiation ...
>
> My Lords, the universality of Communism was, he said, always the greater loyalty. He added that the Chinese found that inadmissible.
>
> Mr Chou en-Lai's explanation tallies very closely with Mr Brezhnev's definition of détente. It is a – and I quote – 'state

of continuing confrontational struggle, which may well need to be intensified'.

My Lords, there, in a nutshell is the democracies' dilemma. None of us could think like that. None of us could talk like that, while, to a Russian negotiator there is nothing inconsistent in that attitude at all. The ideology comes first.

For the democracies the question is always and insistently posed: how, when the ideology of the fellow on the other side of the table insists that he encompass the destruction of your way of life, is it possible to think and to talk in terms of trust? That is basically what all this is about.

It is difficult to imagine Carrington speaking at length in such terms. As he has grown older he has become more surely a man of diplomatic technique and less a man of policy.

It is a good rule, in foreign policy, to attend to the potential power of a possible enemy rather than to his declared intentions. But intentions are never irrelevant: it was Churchill's constant plea to his fellow British politicians in the 1930s that they should read what Adolf Hitler had promised to do as well as studying his actions and considering the elements in the mighty machine of war he was assembling. The difficulty, of course, for a modern Western diplomat, is to take seriously the declared intentions of the Soviet Union, even when they are backed by action in fields as far apart as the North Sea and Afghanistan. The idea that all negotiations should be from strength has yet to sink into the collective mind of Western statesmen: one has only to examine in a cursory fashion the incomprehension which, in Europe and the United States alike, greeted both Mrs Thatcher's early warnings against Soviet imperialism and President Reagan's resolute determination to refurbish American military capacity before he would begin seriously to consider the desirability of negotiating the details of military disengagement with the USSR to see the extent to which reality had departed from the considerations most favoured in Western councils.

Carrington could, like his contemporaries in democratic states, readily denounce, in February 1980, the Russian invasion of Afghanistan. In the same month, however, he canvassed with Herr Genscher, the West German Foreign Minister, proposals for an EEC mission to

Moscow, the object of which would be by words alone to persuade the Soviet government to sanction the establishment in that unhappy country of a genuinely neutral government. There was never any prospect of the government in Moscow giving serious consideration to that proposal, unsupported as it was by anything except goodwill. Carrington was, at the time, chairman of the EEC Council of Foreign Ministers: his proposals, unreal and unlikely of fruition as they were, served only to weaken the Western response to aggression. To make this judgement is not to suppose that the member states of the Atlantic Alliance could have, with any degree of probability and conviction, responded with serious effect to what Russia was attempting in central Asia. Fulmination and denunciation were the necessary order of the day and words were, in general, the only and paltry weapons to hand. Most continental European and American diplomats understood how weak the position of the Alliance was, and how little could be done in practical terms to counter Soviet determination to crush the political life out of an ancient people. The difference between Carrington and his contemporaries in the early weeks of 1980 lay in his perfectly sincere belief that words could effect the issue and their conviction that they could not.

The inadequacy and ineffectiveness of the tradition of policy which he represents rests on the assumption that all competitors in the harsh world of international politics are, at bottom, similar in aspiration to oneself, and, for all that their style and mode of expression may be cruder than one's own, possessed by similar hopes and, even, similar dreams. The unrelenting and sustained character of Lord Home's analysis of the Russian diplomatic character and of Soviet intentions is something quite foreign to Carrington's character. To be sure, as I have already said, he is capable in flashes of defining the intentions and the motives of opposing powers; but his comprehension of those motives and intentions is a fitful one. It could not be otherwise, given the deeply rooted nature of his attitude to foreign policy.

'One or two noble lords', he told the Upper House in their debate on the Franks report

> have queried my resignation. Those of your Lordships who
> have longish memories may perhaps recollect an interview I
> gave the night I resigned. In the course of that interview I

said that, given the information we had at that time, I did not believe that the Government or I had mishandled the situation, or that we should have done differently. Nine months later, and with the benefit of the Franks Committee, I do not really honestly think that I can say that I would have done anything of substance differently. But there was an undeniable feeling in this country that Britain's honour and dignity had been affronted. The governor of a British territory had been forcefully removed. An alien flag had been raised over an occupied population. The wide sense of outrage and impotence was understandable, and I was at the head of the Foreign Office. It did not seem to me a time for self-justification and certainly not to cling to office. I think the country is more important than oneself.

This is a statement which has elements of real dignity about it. But there is a plaintive note in it that is unmistakable and, indeed, typical. Carrington has the capacity, which can only be found in a man possessed of exceptional self-assurance, to express both regret and the total lack of it in perfect balance one with another. The capacity for self-deception of a man who can address himself to the subject of a policy that has failed and still insist that nothing seriously wrong was done in the formulation of that policy clearly possesses an enviable personal armour or, perhaps more bluntly, a very thick skin. It remains to be seen how all this will affect the esteem so readily accorded him, in retrospect, as a Foreign Secretary, and, in the future, as a Secretary-General of NATO.

INDEX

Abbott, Stephen 97
Adamson, Campbell 102
Admiralty 64–70, 170
Afghanistan 27, 117, 173
Agriculture, Ministry of 54–9, 65, 170
Aitken, Sir Maxwell (Lord Beaverbrook) 6
Alexander, Andrew 37
Allen-Mills, Tony 20–1
Amery, Julian 26, 145
Amory, Derek Heathcoat 59, 61
appeasement 132–3
Arab
  -Israeli war (1973) 100–1
  powers 16–17
  see also Israel; Middle East
Argentina 7, 14–15, 17–41, 118, 122,
    126–8, 135–6, 159, 162, 167, 171
armed services 114
Art of the Possible, The 49n
Asquith, H. H. 51
Atkins, Humphrey 32–4, 36, 40
Atlantic Alliance see NATO
Attlee 51n
Attlee, Clement 49–51, 53–4, 56, 133
Australia 63, 142, 146
  Governor General 84, 87
  High Commissioner Pl. 1; 7–8, 12, 44,
    61–4
  -New Zealand Bank 43, 44, 84

Baldwin, Stanley 2, 37, 55, 120, 132,
    137–8
Balfour, Arthur 119–20
Barber, Anthony (Lord Barber) 47, 96, 99,
    106–7, 162
Barnes, Dr John 2
Battle for the Falklands, The 21n
Belize 154
Benn, Tony (Lord Stansgate, Anthony
    Wedgwood Benn) 6
Berrill, Sir Keith 124
Bevin, Ernest 115–16
Biffen, John 34
Blake, George 66, 70
Blakenham, Lord 71
Body, Richard 99

Bonar Law, Andrew 87, 132
Boundary Commissioners 82–3
Bruce-Gardyne, Jock 99n
Burgess, Guy 66, 70
Butler, David 4, 79, 96n, 109n
Butler, R. A. 3n, 49, 49n, 72–5, 100

Callaghan, James 21, 34, 83
Campbell-Bannerman, Sir Henry 44, 131
Carr, Robert (Lord Carr of Hadley) 97, 106
Carrington, Charles 43–4, 63
Carrington, Peter (sixth baron)
  ambitions 4–7, 12, 46–9, 75–6, 85, 92,
    112–13, 119, 134
  Appeal 79–80, 84, 96, 98
  appointments 12
    Australia-New Zealand Bank,
      Chairman 43, 44, 84
    Conservative Party, Chairman 79, 92,
      98–9, 106, 170
    Council of Foreign Ministers, EEC,
      Chairman 174
    de Havillands, management trainee 48
    First Lord of the Admiralty 64–70,
      170
    Foreign Secretary 3–5, 9–10, 12–15,
      16–41, 92, 112–14, 119, 126–7,
      129, 135, 137–8, 142–4, 146–53,
      156–60, 167–8, 170–1, 175
    General Electric Company,
      Chairman 162
    High Commissioner to Australia 61–4
    House of Lords whip 49, 50, 54
    Leader of the House of Lords 3, 4, 15,
      44, 45, 49–50, 71, 75, 86, 112
    Opposition Leader of the House of
      Lords Pl. 3; 4, 75–9, 82–5, 170
    Parliamentary Secretary, Ministry of
      Defence 60–2
    Parliamentary Under Secretary,
      Ministry of Agriculture 54–9, 65,
      170
    Questions of Policy Committee,
      Chairman 84, 88–92
    Secretary-General, NATO Pl. 15; 9,
      14, 17, 48, 156, 164–75

Carrington–*cont.*
    Secretary of State for Defence 13, 15,
      63, 85–7, 92–4, 106, 121
    Shadow Cabinet Pl. 4; 9
  army service 9, 12, 15, 42, 45–6
  attitudes to
    Commonwealth 63–4, 80, 142, 144,
      153, 157
    Conservative Party 8, 16, 34, 48,
      78–80, 98–9, 126
    defence 48, 92–4, 165–6, 168, 170–5
    economic policies 9, 11, 44, 98
    EEC 12, 16–18, 21–3, 27–8, 38–9, 78,
      97, 126, 155–8
    Falklands 5, 7, 16–41, 127–9, 135–8,
      159, 162–3
    foreign affairs 3–5, 9–10, 12–41, 92,
      112, 113–14, 119, 126–7, 129, 135,
      137–8, 142–4, 146–53, 156–60,
      164–75
    House of Lords 6, 9, 15, 45, 47, 82, 85
    Middle East 16–19, 24, 29, 31, 100–1
    NATO Pl. 6; 12, 14, 17–18, 61, 78,
      92–3, 164–75
    Poland 27
    press 66, 68–70
    Rhodesia 8, 83, 85, 142–4, 146–8,
      149–53
    social issues 46–8, 50, 60, 96
    Soviet Union 12–13, 27–8, 37–40, 48,
      61–2, 66–70, 112, 121, 165, 166,
      171
    trade unions 97–8
    USA 14, 16, 22, 155, 156–7, 160, 164,
      167–71, 173–4
  Defence Procurement Executive 93
  early life 12, 42–7
  family 42–4
  general election of February 1974 3, 4,
    17, 37, 48, 100–12
  personality and political style 8–11, 27,
    36–7, 61, 69, 79, 85, 90–2, 119, 150,
    156, 158–61, 166–8, 171–5
  relationships with
    colleagues 91–2, 156–7, 166
    Heath 84–5, 94–100, 104–12, 156
    Macmillan 60–1, 70
    Thatcher 9–11, 22–3, 32–41, 44, 112,
      121–2, 144, 146, 148, 155–6,
      158–60, 163
  resignation over Falklands War 135–6,
    162
CBI (Confederation of British
  Industry) 102

Chalfont, Lord 25, 128
Chamberlain, Austen 87n
Chamberlain, Neville 132–3
Changing Anatomy of Britain, The 116n
Churchill, Randolph 2n
Churchill, Winston 1–4, 6, 49, 54–61, 65,
  73, 108, 133, 173
CIA (Central Intelligence Agency) 25, 30
Clarke, Sir Andrew, QC 57
CND (Campaign for Nuclear
  Disarmament) 62
Common Agricultural Policy 157
Common Market *see* EEC
Commonwealth, British 63–4, 78, 80, 140,
  142, 144, 153, 157
  Office 116
  Prime Ministers' conferences:
    (1957) 63–4; (1979) 143, 145, 154
Conquest, Dr Robert 155
Conservative
  Central Office 79, 89, 96–9, 106–7, 110
  governments
    1951–6 54–74, 139, 143
    1970–4 78, 94–110, 158
    1979–83 *see* Thatcher, Margaret
    1983– 163
  Party 8, 16, 34, 48, 78–80, 87n, 98–9,
    126
    Advisory Committee 78
    Chairman 79, 92, 98–9, 106, 170
    conferences Pls. 8, 10; 70, 81
    'conscience of' 35
    electoral machinery 89–92
    foreign policy 78
    fundraising 79–80
    in opposition 50–5, 76–9, 87
    leadership changes: (1963) 3–5, 70–1,
      81; (1975) 4, 37, 47, 75, 81, 112
    Monday Club 80
    postwar reconstruction 49–50, 54, 60
    Questions of Policy committee 84,
      88–92
    rebels 59
    'wartime generation' 46–8
  Research Department 49, 89, 92n, 97
Corfield, Sir Frederick 102
Costa Mendes, Nicanor 29, 30
CPRS *see* Think Tank
Crichel Down affair 37, 55–9, 65, 77
Crossman, Richard 7–8, 53, 65, 85, 96
Curzon, George (Marquis of Kedleston) 1,
  5, 115, 119–20, 132
Curzon: the last phase 1, 5n, 119n
Cyprus 73–4

Daily Express 68, 98
Daily Mail 37, 68
Daily Mirror 35
Daily Sketch 68
Daily Telegraph 20, 159
Davies, Ian 141n
Davis, John 112
Day, Robin 111
Deedes, William 20–1, 71
defence 48, 92–4, 130–2, 165–6, 168, 170–5
Defence, Ministry of 13, 15, 60–2, 65, 85–7, 92–4, 106, 114, 121
    see also NATO
Defence Procurement Executive 93
Defence White Paper (1955) 62
de Gaulle, Charles 23, 60, 166
de Havillands 48
Denktash, Raul 74–5
Dilhorne, Lord 71
diplomacy 116–19, 124–5, 131–2, 135–8, 139, 153, 154, 159–61, 173–4
disarmament 165–6
Disraeli, Benjamin 44
Donnelly, Desmond 76
Douglas-Home, Sir Alec (Lord Home) Pl. 9; ix, 3–4, 5, 7, 9, 71–3, 74–5, 81, 106, 142, 153, 171, 174
du Cann, Edward 99
Dugdale, Sir Thomas (Lord Crathorne) 54–9
Duncan, Sir Val 116, 117, 124
Dutch, and oil crisis of 1973 100–1

Economist, The 128, 129
Eden, Sir Anthony 61, 115, 116, 132–4, 136, 157
Edward VIII 44
EEC Pl. 13; 12, 16–18, 21–3, 27–8, 38–9, 40, 78, 97, 103, 122, 124, 126, 130, 138, 139, 142, 154–8, 160, 166, 173–4
Egypt 133–4
Elizabeth II, Queen 88, 104, 108, 143, 154
Empire, British 116–17, 123, 139–40, 157; *see also* Commonwealth
Energy, Department of 107–8
espionage 65–70, 170
Eton 12, 42
European Parliament 155

Falkender, Marcia 80n, 89n
Falkland Islands
    Emergency Committee 25–6

Franks Report 66, 121–2, 126–9, 163, 174–5
sovereignty, issue of 15, 114, 118, 122, 126–8, 135, 138, 160, 167
War 3, 7, 9, 14, 17–41, 63, 125, 126–9, 134–8, 152, 154, 162–3, 171
Falkland Islands Review: a report of a committee of Privy Counsellors 127n, 129, 159n, 163n
Falkland, Lord 122
Faulkner, Brian 105
First World War, and Foreign Office policies 131–2, 136, 169
Fisher, Nigel 3n, 59n, 61, 64, 94n
Fitt, Gerry 105
Foot, Michael 82
Foreign Office 9–10, 112–38, 159–61, 163
    criticism of 115–16, 124–5, 127–30
    and Falkland War 126–9, 135–8, 159–60; *see also* Falkland Islands
    relationship with Prime Minister 125–6, 129–38, 144, 146, 153–4, 156, 158–61
    and Rhodesia 142–54
    see also Carrington, Peter; diplomacy
Foreign Policies of the Powers, The 139, 159
foreign policy, British 114–15, 121–6, 154, 159–61, 173
Foster, Reginald 68
Franks, Lord 128, 159, 162–3
    report 66, 121, 126–9, 163, 174–5
Fraser, Malcolm 142, 146
Fraser, Sir Hugh (Lord Fraser of Allander) 6, 47

Galbraith, Tam 67, 68
Galtieri, General Leopoldo Fortunato 17, 19, 24–5, 27, 29, 33, 34
Gandhi, Indira Pl. 12
GATT (General Agreement on Tariffs and Trade) 45–6
general elections
    1945 49
    1950 54
    1951 49, 54
    1964 72–5
    1966 76, 78, 81
    1970 4, 77, 79, 83, 85, 87
    February 1974 3, 4, 11, 37, 48, 100–10, 170
    October 1974 110–11
    1979 12, 28
General Electric Company 162

Genscher, Herr 173
George III, King 43
  V 51
  VI 73
Gilbert, Martin 2
Gilmour, Sir Ian 9, 17, 93
Gormley, Joe 100, 104
Government Communications HQ,
  Cheltenham 24
Gowrie, Lord 7
Grey, Sir Edward 131–2, 136
Grigg, John (Lord Altrincham) 6
Guardian 156
Gursel, General 167

Haig, Alexander 24, 29, 164, 170
Hailsham, Lord 3–5, 51, 71; *see also* Hogg,
  Quintin
Halifax, Lord 133
Hallstein, Professor Walter 166
Hansard 132, 145
Hardinge, Lord 116, 122
Hastings, Max 21n, 25, 29
Hattersley, Roy 113
Healey, Denis 94
Heath, Edward Pl. 8; 4, 7, 11, 14, 26, 37–8,
  40, 46–7, 65, 75–82, 84, 87–112, 115,
  130, 140, 142, 156, 157
Hinsley, F. H. 162
Hitler, Adolf 1, 173
HMS
  Conqueror 20
  Endurance 24, 34
  Spartan 20, 29
  Splendid 20
Hogg, Quintin 3–5, 51, 86
Home Civil Service 115, 125
Hong Kong 40, 154, 160
Hoskyns, Percy 68
Houghton, Douglas (Lord
  Houghton) 90–2
House of Lords Pls 3, 9; 3–4, 6, 49, 71
  reform 7–8, 50–2, 53, 81–5, 87, 94,
    96–7, 170
  role in British government 51–2, 82–4
  whips 49–50, 74
*House of Lords and the Labour government
  1964–1970* 52n
Howe, Sir Geoffrey 47, 97, 163, 169
Hurd, Anthony (Lord Hurd) 54, 57
Hurd, Douglas 11, 46, 54, 109n
Hutchinson, George 75, 112

IMF (International Monetary Fund) 155

incomes policy (1972–4) 98, 100–2, 108
Iran 118
Israel 16–17, 21, 30–1, 121, 134, 159–60
Italy, and Argentina 23–4, 30

Jay, Peter 113–14, 119, 123
Jenkins, Simon 21n, 25, 29
Joint Intelligence Committee 30–2, 129
Jones, Jack 99

Kaunda, Kenneth 141, 143, 145–7, 150,
  152–3
Kavanagh, Denis 4n, 100n, 109n
Kee, Robert 36, 110, 135
Keeler, Christine 68
Kennedy, J. F. 74
Kenyatta, Jomo 148–9
Kershaw, Sir Anthony 95
Kinnock, Neil 47
Kristol, Irving 18n, 169n

Labour
  governments
    1945–51 50–4
    1964–70 75–7, 80–4, 170
    1974–9 21, 34, 113, 162
  Party 47–8, 50, 74, 80, 90, 107, 110–11
Lambton, Lord (Earl of Durham) 6
Lancaster House Conference 13–14, 119,
  146–51
Lansdowne, Lord 116, 131
La Prensa 29–30, 126
Latin America 28, 121
Leach, Henry, First Sea Lord 20, 31–2, 33
Lennox-Boyd, Alan (Lord Boyd) 143
Lever, Lord 162
Liberal
  government (1906–16) 131
  Party 44, 51, 110, 111
life peers 81
Lloyd George, David 87n, 120, 132
Lloyd, Selwyn 134
Loreburn, Lord 131
Luce, Richard 24, 28–9, 34, 36, 40, 128
Luns, Dr Josef Pl. 7; 163, 165, 171
Lynch, Jack 23

McClean, Iona 46
Macdonald, Malcolm 64
McGahey, Mick 100
Machel, Samora 147, 150, 152
Maclean, Donald 66, 70
Macleod, Iain 47, 49

Macmillan, Harold 3, 5, 7, 21, 26, 53, 59–71, 80–1, 93, 105, 139, 141–2, 144, 157, 158
Makarios, Archbishop 74–5
Making of British Foreign Policy, The 139
Mallaby, Sir George 64
Malta 46, 73–5
Margach, James 67
Mars-Jones, W. L., QC 68
Marten, Lieutenant-Commander George 57–8, 65
Marten, Neil 99
Maudling, Reginald 38, 40, 49, 104–5, 112
Menendez, General 31
Menzies, Sir Robert 63
Middle East 16–19, 24, 29, 31, 100–1, 117, 118, 122
Middlemas, Professor Keith 2
Milmo, Helenus, QC 68
miners' strike 48, 100–4
Mintoff, Dom Pl. 7; 46, 73–5
Montagu, Victor (Earl of Sandwich) 6
Moran, Lord 58n, 73
Morgan, Dr Janet 7n, 52, 65, 82n, 85n
Morrison, Herbert 115
Mozambique 147, 152
Mrs Thatcher's First Administration: the prophets confounded 99n
Mugabe, Robert 14, 118–19, 141, 145–51
Mugabe, Sally 142
Mulholland, Brendan 68
Mussolini, Benito 133
Muzorewa, Bishop Abel 118, 141–50, 152–3

Nairn, Sir Patrick 162
Nasser, President 133–4
nationalisation 50, 52, 55–8, 76
NATO (North Atlantic Treaty Organisation) Pls 6, 15; 9, 12, 14, 17–18, 46, 48, 61–3, 73–4, 78, 92–3, 117, 138, 141, 154, 156, 163–75
NATO Review 164n
NATO's Strategy: a case of outdated priorities? 93n
Nicolson, Sir Harold 1, 5, 119n
Nkomo, Joshua 118, 141, 144, 147–52
Nkrumah, Kwame 63
Northedge, F. S. 139, 157, 159
Northern Ireland *see* Ulster
North Sea oil 101, 107
Nott, John 9, 20, 32–6, 39
nuclear weapons 62, 94, 168–70
Nugent, Richard 54–5

NUM (National Union of Mineworkers) 100–6
Nyerere, Julius 152

Oldfield, Sir Maurice 21, 27
OPEC (Organisation of Petroleum Exporting Countries) 100–1
Owen, Dr David 8, 34, 113, 121, 123, 126

Pakistan 116–17
Pallister, Sir Michael 128
Palmerston, Lord 123
Panorama 111, 135
Papadopoulos, Colonel 167
Parsons, Sir Anthony 125
Pay Board 102
peers
    and government office 4, 6–7, 71
    and Labour Party 54
    life 81
    resigning titles to stand for elections 3, 5–6, 53, 71
Peron, General Juan 30
Peyton, John 47
Philby, Kim 70
Pincher, Chapman 66
Pinto-Duschinsky, Michael 79, 96n
Pitt, William, the Younger 43
Plaid Cymru 111
Plowden, Lord 116, 124
Poland 27
Pompidou, Georges 130
Poole, Lord 71
Portland spies 66–70
Powell, J. Enoch 35, 40, 47, 49, 73, 82, 88n, 103, 103n, 104, 108, 110
Power and the Pursuit of Peace 162
press 66, 68–70, 87. 129
Prior, James 47, 95, 98, 106
Profumo, John 68, 70
Pym, Francis 105, 112, 113, 129

Radcliffe Commission Pl. 2; 66–9
Radcliffe, Lord 66–9, 170
Reagan, Ronald 16, 18, 33, 155–6, 160, 164, 173
Red Star 35
Rees, Merlyn 162
Rhodesia Pls 10, 14; 8, 13–14, 63, 77–8, 80–3, 87, 96, 118, 140–54, 170–2
    constitutional conference 13–14, 119, 145–52
    see also Zimbabwe
Richey, Colonel George 93n, 94, 165n

Riddell, Peter 87n
Riding the Storm 1956–1959 64
Ridley, Nicholas 25–6, 128
Robinson, Derek 102
Rogers, General Bernard 168, 170
Rose, Richard 50n
Rouca, Senor Iglesias 126
Rowland, 'Tiny' 149
Rowlands, Edward 25
Royal Marines 34
Ryder, Richard 39, 155

St Aldwyn, Lord 71
Salazar, Oliviera 167
Salisbury, third Marquis 116, 117, 120
  fifth Marquis 52, 53, 54, 77
Sampson, Anthony 116n
Sandhurst 42
Sandys, Duncan 94
Scargill, Arthur 100
Schlaudemann, Harry 29
Schmidt, Dr Helmut Pl. 5
Scott, Sir George 120, 123, 153
Scottish Nationalists 107, 111
SDI (Strategic Defence Initiative) (Star
  Wars) 168–70
Second World War, and political
  attitudes 47–8, 133
security services 66–70
Seldon, Anthony 55n, 58n
Shore, Peter 26
Sitole, Ndabininge 141, 147, 150
Smith, David 141n
  Ian 8n, 77, 80, 83, 118, 140–8, 150–2
  Robert 42–4
  Thomas 42
Soames, Lord 119, 149
South Africa 140, 145–7, 150–1
South Georgia 32
Soviet Union 12–13, 27–8, 37–40, 48,
  61–2, 66–70, 112, 117, 118, 121, 137,
  141, 149, 165–6, 170, 171, 173–4
Spaak, Paul-Henri 61
Suez crisis 14, 31, 133–4, 136
Sunday Telegraph 113, 114, 121n
Sunday Times 67
Switzerland, independence of 159

Talleyrand, Charles de 138
Task Force 3, 20, 33–4, 36, 134
Taylor, Peter 113
  Teddy 40
  Vanessa 91n
Tebbit, Norman 113

Tekere, Edgar 145
Thatcher, Dennis 146
Thatcher Government, The 87n
Thatcher, Margaret 3, 4, 8–14, 16, 20–8,
  31–41, 44, 47, 50, 62, 78, 81, 100–1,
  112, 115, 121, 122, 125, 129–30,
  136–8, 139–61, 163, 164, 169, 173
Think Tank (Central Policy Review
  Staff) 116, 117, 124
Thorneycroft, Peter 66, 68, 69
Thorpe, Jeremy 108, 110
Times, The 39
trade unions 97–8, 100–2, 104–6, 109
Tucker, Geoffrey 96

Ulster 105–6, 108
  Unionists 111
Underwater Weapons Establishment *see*
  Portland spies
United Nations 77, 80–1, 83, 140, 144,
  146, 154
Uruguay 30
USA 14, 16, 22, 118, 155–8, 160, 164–71,
  173–4

Valetta, Archbishop of 74
Vansittart, Sir Robert 133
Vassal, John 67–70
  scandal 37, 65–70, 77
Victoria and Albert Museum 12
Vietnam boat-people 40

Walker, Peter 106, 111
Wallenberg, Mrs Raoul 39–40
Walls, General Peter 145–6, 150
Watkinson, Lord 162
'Welfare State' politics 47–50, 60
Whitelaw, William 11, 46–7, 105–11
Whitney, Ray 34
Williams, Tom 56, 58
Wilson, Harold 50, 53, 72, 74–7, 80–5, 87,
  91, 94–6, 107–10, 115, 140, 142
Wilson, Sir Horace 133
*Winston Churchill: the struggle for survival
  1940–1965* 58
Wyatt, Woodrow 76

Young, Lord 7

Zambia 141, 147, 152
Zimbabwe Pl. 14; 13–14, 118; *see also*
  Rhodesia
Zvobgo, Edison 148